Inhalt

Vorwort

Lösungen zu den Übungsaufgaben

Lösungen zu den schriftlichen Abschlussprüfungsaufgaben

Autorinnen und Autoren:
Übungsaufgaben: Brigitte Katzer, Gerhard Philipp und Redaktion
Lösungen Abschlussprüfungen: Tamara Roßdeutsch

Vorwort

Liebe Schülerin, lieber Schüler,

in diesem Lösungsband zu „Original-Prüfungen und Training Realschulabschluss 2024 – Englisch – Hessen" (Best.-Nr. D06150) findest du von unseren Autorinnen und Autoren ausführlich ausgearbeitete und kommentierte Lösungen zu den Übungsaufgaben und zu den vom hessischen Kultusministerium zentral gestellten Original-Prüfungsaufgaben des Realschulabschlusses.

Versuche stets, jede Aufgabe zunächst selbstständig zu lösen, und sieh nicht gleich in der Lösung nach. Solltest du jedoch nicht weiterkommen, kann ein Blick in die Lösung hilfreich sein, da dort wichtige Hinweise zur Bearbeitung der Aufgabe gegeben werden. Am Schluss solltest du deine Lösung in jedem Fall mit der Lösung in diesem Buch vergleichen. Hast du eine Aufgabe nicht richtig gelöst, lohnt es sich, sie sich zu einem späteren Zeitpunkt noch einmal vorzunehmen.

Arbeite alle Aufgaben auf diese Weise Schritt für Schritt durch, dann kann dir in der Prüfung niemand mehr etwas vormachen!

Viel Erfolg!

A Listening Comprehension

*Hinweis: Der „Listening Comprehension Test" besteht aus drei Teilen. Den bei-
den Telefongesprächen in Teil 1 und den Interviews in Teil 2 und 3 sind jeweils Auf-
gabenformate zugeordnet, die in Abschlussprüfungen häufig vorkommen. Bevor du
die einzelnen Texte hörst, hast du Zeit, dich mit der jeweiligen Aufgabenstellung vertraut zu machen.*

Part One

*Hinweis: Zu jedem Gespräch werden dir vier Satzanfänge mit drei möglichen
Satzenden vorgegeben. Deine Aufgabe ist es, das jeweils richtige Satzende zu finden.
Lies dir die Satzanfänge und Wahlmöglichkeiten genau durch, damit du beim Hören
weißt, worauf du achten musst. Beachte, dass auch die falschen Satzenden im Text in
einem anderen Zusammenhang vorkommen können.*

Dialogue 1

a) Sophie Burns wants to book a hotel room
- ☐ near Waverley Station.
- ☑ in Edinburgh.
- ☐ in Breckenridge.

Hinweis: "The Old Waverley Hotel, Edinburgh." (Z. 1/2)

b) Her parents
- ☑ married 25 years ago.
- ☐ know about the trip.
- ☐ married on 15th August.

*Hinweis: Gleich mehrere Textstellen helfen dir, die richtige Lösung zu finden:
"Oh wow, your parents have been married for 25 years!" (Z. 7/8) Die Äußerung
des Hotelangestellten ist eine Antwort auf Sophies Aussage, dass sie ihre Eltern
zur Silberhochzeit, die man nach 25 Ehejahren feiert, mit einem Hotelaufenthalt
überraschen möchte: "I'd like to book a hotel room for my parents for their
silver wedding anniversary." (Z. 4–6)*

1

c) The hotel
   - ☐ room costs £ 165 per person.
   - ☑ is nearly booked out.
   - ☐ room is small, but you can see the castle from there.

   🖉 **Hinweis:** *"We've just had a cancellation. There's only one room left."*
   (Z. 17/18)

d) The hotel
   - ☐ has got a special offer only for December.
   - ☐ offers breakfast, lunch and dinner.
   - ☑ has got a special online offer.

   🖉 **Hinweis:** *"we've got a special offer for online bookings for the winter months."*
   (Z. 27/28)

Dialogue 2

a) Millie Croft
   - ☐ wants to fly to Atlanta.
   - ☑ works for an airline.
   - ☐ wants to complain about a booking.

   🖉 **Hinweis:** *Millie Croft arbeitet im Callcenter einer Fluggesellschaft: "Good afternoon. This is Millie Croft speaking. How may I help you?" (Z. 1/2) Sie nimmt den Anruf von Grace Arnold entgegen, die nach Atlanta fliegen möchte.*

b) The caller
   - ☐ booked a flight three hours ago.
   - ☐ has booked plane tickets for $ 30.
   - ☑ has booked three tickets.

   🖉 **Hinweis:** *"I booked flights with your airline about two hours ago. I just got the bill for <u>three tickets</u> via email. However, the price on the invoice is $30 higher than the one given online." (Z. 3–7)*

c) The booking number is
   - ☐ WYAZ – 3566.
   - ☐ WVEZ – 3566.
   - ☑ WYEZ – 3566.

   🖉 **Hinweis:** *"Do you have the booking number at hand? – Yes. It's WYEZ – 3566." (Z. 10/11)*
   Denke daran, dass im amerikanischen Englisch der Buchstabe „z" [zi:] ausgesprochen wird. In „British English" würde man ihn [zed] aussprechen.

d) The price online and on the bill differs

☐ because the caller does not have a service card.

☐ because it costs $10 to book a seat in advance.

☑ because the caller booked more comfortable seats.

Hinweis: *"you booked seats with extra leg space and that's $10 per person."* (Z. 21/22) Die Kundin hat eine sogenannte „service card", mit der sie kostenlos Sitzplätze reservieren kann. Versehentlich hat sie jedoch Sitze mit mehr Beinfreiheit gebucht. Daher kommt die zusätzliche Gebühr von 30 $.

Part Two

Hinweis: In diesem „listening text" werden sieben Schüler zum Thema Nebenjob befragt. Anhand ihrer Äußerungen musst du die Gedankenblasen A–H den richtigen Personen zuordnen und in die Tabelle eintragen. Eine Gedankenblase bleibt bei dieser Matching-Aufgabe übrig.

Lexi	Marc	Leo	Freya	Riley	Lucas	Hollie
E	H	B	A	F	C	D

Hinweise:

zu Lexi: *"I'm a babysitter."* (Z. 9); *"I look after our neighbours' children. They're two, five and eight years old."* (Z. 13–15)

zu Marc: *"I don't have a part-time job right now. I used to work for a pizza delivery service"* (Z. 16–18); *"My parents made me quit two weeks ago"* (Z. 22)

zu Leo: *"I'm a Maths tutor."* (Z. 24/25); *"My rates are affordable for everyone."* (Z. 26/27)

zu Freya: *"Some of my friends say they'd never want to do my job, but I really like it. For me, it's relaxing."* (Z. 36–38)

zu Riley: *"It's volunteer work, so I don't get paid"* (Z. 43/44)

zu Lucas: *"I've never had a part-time job. [...] both my parents are successful lawyers [...]. Money isn't a problem."* (Z. 46–51)

zu Hollie: *"I started to make my own jewellery and sell it online and at markets. Especially my earrings are a great success. I'm always very happy when I see someone wearing a piece I've made."* (Z. 58–62)

Part Three

Hinweis: *Deine Aufgabe ist es, die folgende Tabelle mit den fehlenden Informationen in Stichpunkten zu vervollständigen. Lies die Aufgabenstellung genau und halte dich an die Vorgaben; so ist es z. B. bei „personal experience with the airline (one aspect)" ausreichend, nur einen Gesichtspunkt zu nennen. Bei „the language(s) she speaks fluently" musst du genau zuhören und dann entscheiden, ob eine oder mehrere Sprachen genannt werden müssen.*

(1) Eileen O'Hara's age	**25 / twenty-five years**
(2) period of time she worked in London	**(for) 3 / three years**
(3) the language(s) she speaks fluently	**English, German**
(4) personal experience with the airline (one aspect)	**(she) felt safe on board / (she) felt well looked after / cabin crew were (very) friendly**
(5) one reason why the job is physically demanding	**cabin crew must be able to stand for a long time / (you) have to lift heavy hand luggage / (you) have to push heavy beverage carts / (you) have to be strong (to lift ... carts)**
(6) the sport she does more than once a week	**running / (she) goes running**
(7) where she would not like to live	**outside Europe**
(8) city where the training for new cabin crew takes place	**Dublin**
(9) number of trainees taking part in the training courses	**20–40 / twenty to forty (trainees)**
(10) period of time the airline will get in touch with Eileen	**(within the next) 4 / four days**

Hinweise:
zu 1: *"Well, I'm 25 years old" (Z. 11)*
zu 2: *"I worked in a big hotel in London for three years." (Z. 13/14)*

zu 3: Eileen, deren Mutter Deutsche ist, ist in Irland aufgewachsen und zweispra-chig erzogen worden. Zwar hat sie Grundkenntnisse in Französisch, spricht die Sprache aber nicht fließend. Da die Frage lautet, welche Sprache(n) sie fließend spricht, musst du „English" <u>und</u> „German" als Lösung angeben: "I speak German fluently […]." (Z. 14/15)

zu 4: "Every time I flew with your airline, I felt safe and well looked after on board. And all the cabin crew were so friendly." (Z. 23–25)

zu 5: "You must be able to stand for a long time; you have to be strong enough to lift heavy hand luggage and push heavy beverage carts." (Z. 38–41)

zu 6: "I run about six kilometres three times a week." (Z. 42/43) Die anderen Sport-arten – Yoga und Krafttraining – betreibt Eileen nur einmal pro Woche.

zu 7: "I wouldn't want to live outside Europe." (Z. 55/56)

zu 8: "The flight attendant training takes place at our airline training centre here in Dublin" (Z. 62–64)

zu 9: "Classes are usually made up of between 20 to 40 trainees" (Z. 67/68)

zu 10: "You'll hear from us within the next four days" (Z. 76/77)

B Reading Comprehension

📎 Hinweis: Im Prüfungsteil Leseverstehen begegnen dir bisweilen recht anspruchs-volle Texte. Lass dich vom Umfang und sprachlichen Niveau dieser Texte nicht ver-unsichern, da du oftmals nicht jedes einzelne Wort verstehen musst, um die gestell-ten Aufgaben zu beantworten. Lies dir die Aufgaben aber immer gut durch, da hier meist mehr Details als in den Hörverstehensaufgaben gefordert werden. Dafür hast du aber auch die Möglichkeit, dir die Texte mehrmals genau durchzulesen.

1. Airline information

📎 Hinweis: Bei dieser Aufgabe sollst du zu den einzelnen Abschnitten (1–5) des Lesetextes über eine Fluggesellschaft passende Überschriften (A–G) finden. Sieh dir vor dem ersten Lesen des Textes die möglichen Überschriften an. Beim Lesen des Textes ist es sinnvoll, Schlüsselwörter zu unterstreichen oder hervor-zuheben. So kannst du dich im Anschluss leichter für die jeweils am besten passende Überschrift entscheiden. Denke daran, dass die Überschriften sich je-weils auf den gesamten Absatz beziehen müssen und nicht nur Teilaspekte ab-decken. Zwei „headings" bleiben übrig.

part of the text	❶	❷	❸	❹	❺
heading	E	B	G	D	C

Hinweise:

zu 1: *Im ersten Absatz des Textes werden allgemeine Informationen über die Fluggesellschaft gegeben, z. B. über die Flugziele, die Anzahl der Angestellten, Flugzeuge und Passagiere: "We operate both domestic and international flights [...]. Our team consists of 4,000 employees [...]. Our fleet comprises 43 planes. We have approximately 10 million passengers per year on board our planes."*

zu 2: *In diesem Absatz geht es um die Sicherheit und um die Freundlichkeit des Personals: "Safety is our main concern. [...] we want to make the flight experience with us special [...]. We want our passengers to leave the plane with a smile and to look forward to flying with us again."*

zu 3: *Der dritte Textabschnitt handelt vom Internetzugang an Bord: "On our transatlantic flights, it is now possible for you to stay connected: Onboard Wi-Fi enables you to browse the internet, email or text your friends"*

zu 4: *Sowohl „luggage" als auch „baggage" bedeuten „Gepäck". Dieser Abschnitt handelt von den neuen Gepäckvorschriften der Fluggesellschaft: "We introduced a new checked baggage policy for inner-European flights"*

zu 5: *Im letzten Absatz geht es um die vielen Eigenschaften, die Flugbegleiter mitbringen müssen, wie z. B. Pünktlichkeit, Zuverlässigkeit, Kreativität: "Are you punctual and reliable? Are you spontaneous and creative when it comes to solving problems? [...] Do you like helping people? Can you listen patiently [...]?" Da Überschrift „A" („Flight attendants – competent in handling difficult situations") nur einen Teilaspekt anspricht, passt Überschrift „C" („Qualities of a flight attendant") am besten.*

2. Angel Air – Cabin Crew (Flight Attendants)

Hinweis: Hier hast du vier Auswahlmöglichkeiten und musst für die Satzanfänge die jeweils passende Satzergänzung finden.

a) The text is

☐ an interview about an airline.

☑ a job offer.

☐ a story about an airline.

☐ a newspaper article about Angel Air.

Hinweis: Bei diesem Text handelt es sich um eine Stellenanzeige. Angel Air sucht Flugbegleiter zur Festanstellung für ihren Standort Dublin. Die Anzeige ist gegliedert in „Job Description" (Z. 1), Hours and Working Conditions"(Z. 28), „Training"(Z. 39), „The Benefits"(Z. 46) und „Application Process and Criteria" (Z. 50).

b) Cabin crew
- [ ] have to be from Dublin.
- [ ] will get a short-term contract.
- [✓] have to make sure the passengers are safe and feel comfortable on board.
- [ ] can also work part-time.

✎ **Hinweis:** *"you welcome our customers aboard the aircraft; <u>their safety</u> <u>and comfort are your responsibility.</u> You will hold the key to our customers having a fantastic flight and, most importantly, wanting to fly with us again."* (Z. 4–7)

c) After take-off, cabin crew
- [ ] check the cabin equipment.
- [ ] make sure the passengers' hand luggage is stored away safely.
- [ ] give a safety demonstration.
- [✓] offer the passengers something to eat and drink.

✎ **Hinweis:** *"During a flight, the crew serve meals and drinks"* (Z. 15)
Die anderen Aufgaben müssen bereits vor dem Start erledigt sein.

d) Angel Air is looking for flight attendants
- [ ] for their only base outside Ireland.
- [ ] for all their bases.
- [ ] only for their Irish bases.
- [✓] only for their base in Dublin.

✎ **Hinweis:** *"However, we are currently only hiring for our base in Dublin."* (Z. 26/27)

e) The airline
- [ ] does not operate on religious holidays.
- [ ] gives flight attendants heavy discounts on duty-free products.
- [ ] wants flight attendants to be proud of their looks.
- [✓] operates all year round.

✎ **Hinweis:** *"As the airline <u>operates 365 days a year,</u> shifts include weekends, nights, public holidays and religious festivals."* (Z. 29/30)

f) Flight attendants do not have to deal with
- [✓] eleven-year-olds travelling alone.
- [ ] dangerous flying conditions.
- [ ] irregular working hours.
- [ ] jet lag and other health problems.

✎ **Hinweis:** *Die Flugbegleiter müssen mit gefährlichen Flugbedingungen, unregelmäßigen Arbeitszeiten, Jetlag und anderen gesundheitlichen Problemen umgehen können (Z. 29–36). In den Zeilen 22–24 findest du zudem den Hinweis, dass sie sich <u>nicht</u> um Kinder zu kümmern brauchen, die jünger als*

7

12 Jahre alt sind: "Cabin crew will sometimes have to pay special attention to minors (ages 12–15) travelling on their own. However, children under the age of 12 are not allowed on board without a guardian."

g) The airline
- ☐ offers applicants one week of training.
- ☐ pays all the cabin crew members € 30,000 per year.
- ☑ asks their cabin crew to take tests on safety regularly.
- ☐ does not organise hotel accommodation on layovers.

✎ **Hinweis:** *"Air cabin crew have to pass regular examinations that test knowledge of safety and emergency procedures to make sure that official first aid requirements are up to date." (Z. 43–45)*

h) Flight attendants
- ☐ are trained in first aid, cabin service and German.
- ☑ can take 30 days off per year.
- ☐ are trained in security procedures and international communication.
- ☐ are tested on first aid before they are allowed to take part in the training course.

✎ **Hinweis:** *"Holiday entitlement is 30 days" (Z. 48)*
Die Flugbegleiter erhalten keinen Deutschunterricht und keine Ausbildung in internationaler Kommunikation. Ihr Wissen über Erste Hilfe wird auch nicht vor dem Beginn des Kurses geprüft.

i) Flight attendants have to be able to
- ☐ speak English and one more language.
- ☐ speak more than two languages.
- ☐ speak and write at least two languages.
- ☑ speak and write at least German and English.

✎ **Hinweis:** *"High standard of written and spoken English and German are required. Other languages will be an advantage." (Z. 51/52)*

k) Before being invited to the training course, applicants
- ☐ only have to fill in the application form.
- ☐ fill in the application form and do a telephone interview.
- ☑ fill in the application form, hand in the required documents and do a telephone interview.
- ☐ fill in the application form, hand in the required documents and do a language test.

✎ **Hinweis:** *"To apply, complete the online application form and send us copies of your [...]. The first stage of the selection procedure is a telephone interview." (Z. 53–58)*

3. Tips for your first day at work

Hinweis: Zu diesem Text musst du Fragen beantworten. Lies dir zuerst die Fragen durch, damit du weißt, worauf du beim Lesen achten sollst. Markiere dann beim Lesen die entsprechenden Textstellen.

a) people who have just found a new job (and had their first day at work)
   Hinweis: "read the following tips that have been posted by people who have just found a job and have survived the first day at the new company." (introduction)

b) Having some background knowledge gives you confidence/prevents you from asking stupid questions.
   Hinweis: "I assure you that you'll be much more confident if you've got some facts and figures about the company at hand. By the way, I didn't read up on the company and asked some really stupid questions ..." (Tip 1)

c) because you meet many new people and get lots of information which you are supposed to remember / because the first day is exhausting
   Hinweis: "The first day at a new job is very exhausting, because you meet a lot of new people who bombard you with lots of information. Do you think you will remember any of it if the only thing you want to do is go back to bed?" (Tip 2)

d) (it is to) be on time / (it is to) test drive the way to work during rush hour and plan for some extra time
   Hinweis: "Be on time"; "Ideally, test drive your route during rush hour – and then plan for some extra time" (Tip 3)

e) He arrived (25 minutes) late, because his bus was stuck in a traffic jam.
   Hinweis: "On my first day, the bus I wanted to take was stuck in a traffic jam and I arrived 25 minutes late." (Tip 3)

f) a few days before your first day at work
   Hinweis: "And decide what you want to wear a few days in advance, so that you could still go shopping if there was an emergency." (Tip 4)

g) She was wearing something too tight/small.
   Hinweis: "I hadn't thought about the clothes issue beforehand, so on the morning of day one I found out that I didn't fit into my office clothes any more. Let me tell you, it's not a good feeling to be wearing something way too tight on your first day" (Tip 4)

h) She took notes (on people's names).
   Hinweis: "What I did is I secretly took notes on my colleagues' names, because I'm really bad at remembering them." (Tip 5)

9

i) They are reading it, because they have probably just found a job and want to prepare for their first day. / ... and are looking for some good advice on what is important on your first day at a new job.

Hinweis: Um diese Frage zu beantworten, musst du zurück zur Einleitung gehen. Du findest die Antwort nicht wortwörtlich im Text, aber einige Text-stellen geben dir Anhaltspunkte, wie du die Frage beantworten kannst: "First of all, congratulations! You've landed a job [...]. If you manage to follow some of the tips, your first day at work will be a piece of cake" (introduction)

C Use of Language

1. Mediation

Hinweis: Bei dieser Aufgabe sollst du in einem Gespräch dolmetschen. Ein Lehrer gibt dir auf Deutsch Informationen vor, die du sinngemäß für einen eng-lischsprachigen Austauschschüler ins Englische übertragen sollst. Anschließend sollst du dessen Antworten und seine Fragen dem Lehrer auf Deutsch mitteilen. Achte immer genau auf die jeweils geforderte Zielsprache – die eckigen Klam-mern vor den Antwortzeilen helfen dir dabei. Du sollst hier nicht alles Wort für Wort übersetzen. Manchmal gibt es mehr als eine Möglichkeit, etwas in der Ziel-sprache auszudrücken.

LEHRER: Kannst du Cameron bitte sagen, dass er am Montag um 8.00 Uhr in der Schule sein soll und dann gleich zum Chemieraum gehen muss.

DU [E]: **On Monday you'll have to be at school by 8 o'clock (in the mor-ning) / 8 a.m. and then go straight to the chemistry lab.**

CAMERON: Yes thanks, I will, but where is the chemistry lab? And what's the teacher's name?

DU [D]: **Er wird zum Chemieraum kommen, weiß aber nicht, wo er sich befindet. Außerdem möchte er wissen, wen er in Chemie hat.**

LEHRER: Er hat bei Frau Müller Chemie. Vielleicht kannst du dich ja hier vor dem Lehrerzimmer mit ihm treffen und dann könnt ihr gemeinsam hingehen? Sag ihm bitte auch, dass das Kaugummikauen bei uns an der Schule verboten ist und wir es auch nicht dulden, dass Mützen im Unterricht getragen werden.

DU [E]: **Mrs Müller's your chemistry teacher. Why don't we meet here in front of the staff room so that I can show you the way? By the way, you aren't allowed to/mustn't chew gum in school or wear a cap in class.**

CAMERON: All right, let's do that. Could you ask if I can use my smartphone in class? It has a dictionary and I don't understand much.

DU [D]:	Er fragt, ob er sein Handy/Smartphone als Wörterbuch benutzen darf, da sein Deutsch noch nicht so gut ist.
LEHRER:	Ja, Cameron darf sein Telefon dafür verwenden, aber auch nur dafür. Er braucht aber eine Sondergenehmigung vom Schulleiter, weil Handys bei uns ja sonst verboten sind. Und er muss bitte den Kollegen selbstständig deswegen Bescheid geben.
DU [E]:	**Yes, you can, but you'll need special permission from the headmaster/principal since it is (strictly) forbidden to use mobile/cell phones in school. Please let your teachers know that you have special permission to use it.**
CAMERON:	All right, I will.
LEHRER:	Sollte er noch weitere Fragen haben, kann er sich jederzeit an mich wenden. Vielen Dank, dass du weitergeholfen hast.
DU [E]:	**If you have any other questions feel free to ask him/Mr Waas.**

2. Words and structures

Hinweis: In diesem Teil werden verschiedene Grammatikaspekte abgeprüft und es wird getestet, wie sicher du deinen Wortschatz beherrschst. Für jede Lücke im Text werden dir vier Antwortmöglichkeiten vorgegeben, von denen du jeweils die richtige auswählst. Wenn du dir bei einer grammatikalischen Form nicht sicher bist oder die Lücke falsch ausgefüllt hast, lies die entsprechenden Regeln in der Kurzgrammatik (auf der Onlineplattform MyStark) noch einmal nach.

❶ ☐ by ☐ in ☐ to ☑ for	❷ ☐ which ☐ then ☑ when ☐ after	❸ ☑ inconvenience ☐ sorry ☐ accident ☐ attention
❹ ☐ walk back ☐ had gone ☐ was running ☑ returned	❺ ☑ for participating in ☐ participating with ☐ to participate in ☐ to take part	❻ ☐ On the end ☐ At the end ☑ Finally ☐ At least
❼ ☑ during ☐ while ☐ for ☐ through	❽ ☐ Not ☑ What ☐ Which ☐ So much	❾ ☑ calm ☐ in a calm way ☐ calmer ☐ calmly
❿ ☐ have you to ☑ are you going to ☐ you will ☐ you go to		

✎ Hinweise:

zu ❶: *Die fehlende Präposition muss ausdrücken, dass jemand „auf etwas war-
tet"; im Englischen ist dies „to wait for sth".*

zu ❷: *Du brauchst hier eine Konjunktion, die den Hauptsatz und den Nebensatz
verbindet. Das Wort „then" fällt daher bereits weg. Auch das Relativpronomen
„which" passt nicht. Da durch den Gebrauch des „past progressive" im Hauptsatz („was waiting") ein vorzeitiger Bezug ausgeschlossen wird, fällt auch
„after" weg. Die Konjunktion „when" hingegen drückt in diesem Fall aus, dass
eine längere Handlung, nämlich das Warten an Gate 35, durch die Durchsage
unterbrochen wird.*

zu ❸: *Der Sprecher der Durchsage entschuldigt sich für etwas („We apologise
for ...“). Das Wort „inconvenience" bedeutet „Unannehmlichkeit" und passt
hier zur Situation, im Gegensatz zu den übrigen Wahlmöglichkeiten.*

zu ❹: *Die Verben, die zur Auswahl stehen, sind alles Verben der Bewegung, die
grundsätzlich in diesem Kontext in Frage kommen würden. Allerdings ist hier
nur „returned" möglich, da es sich um eine Abfolge mehrerer Handlungen in der
Vergangenheit handelt, die den Gebrauch des „simple past" verlangt.*

zu ❺: *Bei dieser Lücke sind gleich zwei Dinge zu beachten. Zum einen musst du
wissen, dass „to thank" die Präposition „for" verlangt. Zum anderen musst du
gelernt haben, dass „to participate" mit der Präposition „in" steht. Lerne am
besten beide Ausdrücke auswendig: „to thank sb for doing sth" und „to participate in sth".*

zu ❻: *Das Adverb „schließlich" hat im Englischen folgende Entsprechungen:
„finally", „at last" und „in the end". Da hier nur „finally" zur Wahl steht, ist
das die richtige Lösung.*

zu ❼: *„Während" kann im Englischen durch „during" oder „while" ausgedrückt werden. „While" ist jedoch eine Konjunktion, die einen Nebensatz ein-
leitet. In diesem Satzzusammenhang wird hingegen eine Präposition benötigt, die
sich auf „the flight" beziehen kann. Daher kommt nur „during" als Lösung
infrage.*

zu ❽: *„Was für eine blöde Frage" heißt im Englischen „What a stupid question".*

zu ❾: *Das Verb „to stay" ist ein sogenanntes „linking verb". Es schließt ein Adjektiv und kein Adverb an. Die Grundform des Adjektivs „calm" ist hier die einzig mögliche Lösung.*

zu ❿: *Du kannst hier sofort erkennen, dass es sich um eine Frage handelt, die im
Englischen eine besondere Wortstellung erfordert. Die Optionen „you will" und
„you go to" passen somit nicht in die Lücke. Ebenso würde „have you to" eine
Umschreibung mit „do" benötigen. Da es sich zudem um einen Plan für die Zukunft handelt, benötigt man das „going to-future": „What are you going to do?"*

D Text Production

*✦ **Hinweis:** In der Textproduktion kannst du zwischen zwei Themen wählen. Lies zuerst beide Themen aufmerksam durch und überlege genau, welches dir mehr liegt. Insgesamt sollst du einen Text von rund 150 Wörtern verfassen. Achte beim Schreiben darauf, dass du die Vorgaben der Aufgabenstellung berücksichtigst. Lies am Ende noch einmal deinen ganzen Text konzentriert durch. Korrigiere dabei Grammatik- und Rechtschreibfehler. Überprüfe auch, ob dein Text logisch aufgebaut ist. Die Beispiellösungen sind etwas länger als die geforderten 150 Wörter, da hier auf alle Aspekte eingegangen wird. Du brauchst in deiner Antwort aber nur auf vier der fünf Fragen antworten.*

What is the story behind the picture?

I remember the day as if it were yesterday. It was my brother's 18th birthday and the first day of our summer holiday. We had just landed in San Francisco, where we wanted to spend the first few days of our three-week-long trip. My parents had saved for us to go on such a spectacular holiday for a very long time, so we were really excited. My brother was especially excited, because he is an expert on planes and knows everything!

When the "fasten your seat-belt sign" was switched off, we were ready to leave the plane, but suddenly, there was another announcement. "We would kindly ask Linus and Noah Meier to come to the cockpit before leaving the plane." What's going on? Linus looked at me and shrugged. Our parents also looked confused but told us to do what we had been asked. We went to the front of the plane and were greeted by the pilot and co-pilot, who congratulated my brother. They then asked us if we wanted to see the cockpit. What a question – of course! My brother asked a million questions and the pilots patiently answered them all. I didn't understand very much, so I took this photo.

203 words

School will be over soon – what now?

My name is Mia Becker and I will take my GCSEs in six months' time. The big question for me and all the other graduates is: What's next? I have thought long and hard about what I would like to do after school. I have talked to my parents, my sister, my friends and my teachers, and everyone has given me some good advice.

However, I have to decide for myself what will be best for me, so before starting work, I'm going to take a gap year. I want to travel the world, meet interesting people from other countries, get to know foreign cultures, improve my English and enjoy life. I also want to use this time to decide in which field I would like to work later on. I know that some employers (and parents) think taking a gap year is a waste of time, but I disagree. I strongly believe that you can grow as a person because you are responsible for all your actions and decisions.

I would like to go to Australia, where I would love to work on a farm in the Outback. It would be a totally new experience for me – I am used to busy life in Frankfurt. A friend of mine has asked me if she can come with me and I told her that I wanted to go alone. To be honest, it would feel much safer to be travelling with someone I know and like, but I have the feeling that I have to do this on my own.   *260 words*

A Listening Comprehension

✐ *Hinweis: Der Prüfungsteil Hörverstehen besteht aus drei Teilen. Den beiden „News Items" in Teil 1 und den Interviews in Teil 2 und 3 sind jeweils Aufgabenformen zugeordnet, die in Abschlussprüfungen häufig vorkommen. Bevor du die einzelnen Texte hörst, hast du Zeit, dich mit der jeweiligen Aufgabenstellung vertraut zu machen.*

Part One

✐ *Hinweis: Zu jedem „News Item" werden vier Satzanfänge mit drei möglichen Enden vorgegeben. Deine Aufgabe ist es, das jeweils richtige Satzende zu finden. Lies die Anfänge und Wahlmöglichkeiten genau durch, damit du beim Hören weißt, worauf du achten musst. Beachte, dass falsche Satzenden im Text in einem anderen Zusammenhang vorkommen können. Versuche, die falschen Optionen auszuschließen.*

News Item 1

a) Thanksgiving is celebrated to remember the
  ☐ foundation of the new colonies.
  ☐ arrival of the first settlers.
  ☑ Pilgrims' first harvest.

  ✐ *Hinweis: "Its origins can be traced back to the time of the <u>Pilgrim Fathers</u> […] who celebrated their <u>first successful harvest</u>." (Z. 2–5)*

b) Harry Truman was the first president
  ☐ who spared a turkey on Thanksgiving.
  ☑ who was given a turkey as a present.
  ☐ who officially celebrated Thanksgiving.

  ✐ *Hinweis: "Harry Truman was the first president to be presented with a turkey as a gift to his family" (Z. 12/13)*

c) The first official pardon was issued by
  ☐ John F. Kennedy.
  ☑ Ronald Reagan.
  ☐ George Bush senior.

  ✐ *Hinweis: "The first time an official pardon was issued took place in 1987, when Ronald Reagan was asked …" (Z. 20–22)*

15

d) Oliver North

☑ was indirectly responsible for the first turkey pardoning.

☐ wanted to become president instead of Reagan.

☐ fought in the Iran War.

✎ *Hinweis: "Ronald Reagan was asked whether he would pardon Oliver North, a man who was engaged in the so-called 'Iran-Contra Affair', a political scandal during Reagan's presidency. As he did not want to answer the question, he preferred to pardon the turkey instead" (Z. 22–27)*

News Item 2

a) Zac Mihajlovic

☐ lives in Austria.

☑ is 29 years old.

☐ was born in 1998.

✎ *Hinweis: "This might be the line of thoughts that crossed <u>29-year-old</u> Australian Zac Mihajlovic's mind a few years ago." (Z. 3–5) Zac lebt nicht in Österreich („Austria"), sondern in Australien, und er ist nicht 1998 geboren, wobei diese Zahl gar nicht im Hörtext vorkommt (vgl. „1989", Z. 8).*

b) He built his Batmobile

☐ with his grandfather.

☐ to fight crime.

☑ in his backyard.

✎ *Hinweis: "He spent two years of his life building an exact copy of the Batmobile shown in the first movie from 1989 in his <u>backyard</u>." (Z. 6–8)*

c) The car is so special because

☐ it has bullet-proof windows.

☐ even a police escort cannot stop it.

☑ it has a real car licence.

✎ *Hinweis: "It took Zac another year to work in all the details needed for a <u>registered car licence</u>. Now the car is not just a life-sized model – it is actually driving with licence plates, papers and all." (Z. 8–12)*

d) Zac needed the police once because

☑ there were people blocking his way.

☐ people took pictures of him in Sydney.

☐ they helped him fight some criminals.

✎ *Hinweis: "Once he even needed a police escort to get out of a place when he was in Sydney with the car." (Z. 18–20)*
Dass die Leute das Auto fotografieren, ist für ihn normal (vgl. Z. 16–18).

Part Two

Hinweis: In diesem „listening text" werden sieben Schüler zum Thema Halloween befragt. Anhand ihrer Äußerungen musst du die Gedankenblasen A–H den richtigen Personen zuordnen und in die Tabelle eintragen. Eine Gedankenblase bleibt bei dieser Matching-Aufgabe übrig.

Karen	Pete	Kira	Eric	Tony	Dave	Mary
D	G	E	H	F	B	C

Hinweise:

zu Karen: "My older brothers, Chris and Michael, are married and have little children. But on Halloween they all come to our house and the whole family enjoys a nice evening together." (Z. 9–13)

zu Pete: "my younger brother is only five, and I look after him when he walks around our neighbourhood." (Z. 20–22); "he shares with me. He always says this is my 'payment' for helping him. That's funny!" (Z. 23–25)

zu Kira: Um die Lösung zu finden, musst du etwas zwischen den Zeilen lesen. Kira findet die Dekorationen, die ihre Eltern an Halloween machen „amazing" (Z. 32); ihr Vater baute sogar einen Sarg mit Mumie (vgl. Z. 33–35).

zu Eric: "Did you know that Halloween is an old special Celtic tradition?" (Z. 37/38)

zu Tony: "I love candy and on Halloween you can have tons of it." (Z. 48–50); "our family supper on Halloween is legendary." (Z. 51/52)

zu Dave: "I'm sorry, but I don't like Halloween at all." (Z. 55/56)

zu Mary: "I like being creative with my costumes. Every year I come up with something new. It often takes weeks to finish my costume." (Z. 66–69)

Part Three

Hinweis: Deine Aufgabe ist es, die folgende Tabelle mit den fehlenden Informationen in Stichpunkten zu vervollständigen. Lies die Aufgabenstellung genau. Pass besonders bei den Zahlen auf: Manchmal geht es um Zeitabschnitte vor einer bestimmten Jahreszahl („before 2013") und manchmal wird die Zahl im Text nicht explizit genannt, sodass du genau auf den Kontext achten musst. Besonders bei den Aufgaben, bei denen nach dem Grund („reason") gefragt wird, solltest du dir beim Hören Notizen machen.

(1) number of people living in Rochelle, Georgia	**(about) 1,400 (inhabitants)**
(2) where the prom took place the day before	**(at the) (local) high school gym**
(3) organizers of the prom before 2013	**students and parents**
(4) period of time in which proms were racially separated	**(for) (more than) fifty / 50 years**
(5) reason why some students did not want to celebrate separately	**(they) wanted to celebrate with all (of) their friends**
(6) organizers of the integrated prom in 2013	**two black and two white girls**
(7) decade since when African Americans have been allowed at high schools	**(since) the 1960s / sixties**
(8) reason why younger students were not allowed to go to the prom in 2013	**too many people there / there would have been too many people**
(9) Rachel's reaction to her own prom	**she had a great time / she enjoyed herself (a lot)**
(10) Rachel's opinion about young black and white people celebrating together	**perfectly normal / nothing special**

Hinweise:

zu 1: "Rochelle, Georgia, a southern city in the US with about 1,400 inhabitants." (Z. 2–4)

zu 2: "Yesterday [...] a school-sponsored prom was held at the local high school gym." (Z. 4–6)

zu 3: "That means that before 2013 the students and their parents had to organize the event on their own." (Z. 13–16)

zu 4: "these events were usually racially separated. [...] And that did not change for a long period of time – _for more than fifty years_ no one even questioned that habit." (Z. 16–22)

zu 5: "A couple of students didn't want to celebrate separately. They wanted to spend this special evening with all of their friends." (Z. 24–26)

18

zu 6: In diesem Abschnitt geht es um den Ball des Jahres 2013: *"there were two black and two white girls, who were really close friends."* (Z. 29/30); *"They came together and organized a private integrated prom"* (Z. 32/33)

zu 7: *"In the 1960s the first African Americans were allowed to enter high schools that used to be exclusively for white people in those days."* (Z. 36–39)

zu 8: *"younger students weren't allowed to show up because there would have been too many people there."* (Z. 48–50)

zu 9: *"So, Rachel, how was your own prom yesterday? – I had a great time."* (Z. 63–65)

zu 10: *"I believe black and white kids celebrating together should be perfectly normal and nothing special after all."* (Z. 70–73)

B Reading Comprehension

Hinweis: Im Prüfungsteil Leseverstehen begegnen dir bisweilen recht anspruchsvolle Texte. Lass dich vom Umfang und sprachlichen Niveau dieser Texte nicht verunsichern, da du oftmals nicht jedes einzelne Wort verstehen musst, um die gestellten Aufgaben zu beantworten. Lies dir die Aufgaben aber immer gut durch, da hier meist mehr Details als in den Hörverstehensaufgaben gefordert werden. Dafür hast du aber auch die Möglichkeit, dir die Texte mehrmals genau durchzulesen.

1. Theatre reviews

Hinweis: Bei dieser Aufgabe sollst du herausfinden, welche der genannten Personen (1–5) das jeweils passende Theaterstück (A–G) besucht bzw. darin mitwirkt. Hier hilft es, wenn du dir die Beschreibungen 1–5 genau durchliest und Schlüsselwörter unterstreichst oder hervorhebst. Dann weißt du, worauf du beim Lesen der Rezensionen achten musst und es wird dir leichter fallen, die Theaterstücke der jeweiligen Person zuzuordnen. Zwei Stücke passen nicht.

person	❶	❷	❸	❹	❺
play	F	A	G	D	B

Hinweise:

zu ❶: Das Wort „show" wird in den Personenbeschreibungen als allgemeiner Begriff für Theaterproduktion, Oper etc. verwendet und gibt keine Hilfestellung. Jedoch hilft dir der Hinweis, dass die von Helen besuchte Produktion auf Liedern einer Musikgruppe gründet, dabei, die Auswahl einzuschränken (*"based on […] songs by Queen."*). Die entscheidende Information ist der „astrophysi-

cist", *der der „lead guitarist of Queen." ist. Darum kann es sich nur um „We Will Rock You" (F) handeln.*

zu ❷: *Die Kurzbeschreibung des Inhalts deckt sich nur mit der Beschreibung von „Swan Lake" (A): "a princess called Odette, who is turned into a swan by an evil sorcerer's curse."*

zu ❸: *Der eindeutige Hinweis ist hier die Aussage, dass die Schauspieler als Tiere verkleidet sind, denn das trifft nur auf „The Lion King" (G) zu: "because actors are dressed in colourful animal costumes". Diese Aussage ist lediglich in einem Teil eines Nebensatzes zu finden, weswegen sie dir leicht entgehen kann. Lies die Texte also immer ganz genau.*

zu ❹: *Die Beschreibung von Pauls Rolle weist hier im beinahe identischen Wortlaut zwei der vier Eigenschaften der Hauptrolle aus „The Wall" (D) auf: "he lost his father in the Second World War […] and was abandoned by his wife later on."*

zu ❺: *Auch hier musst du die Beschreibung zu „Porgy and Bess" (B) ganz genau lesen, um die relevante Information („a handicapped black man") zu finden – das Adjektiv „handicapped" ist ein Synonym für „disabled".*

2. The history of Halloween

🖋 *Hinweis: Hier hast du vier Auswahlmöglichkeiten und musst für die Satzanfänge die jeweils passende Satzergänzung finden.*

a) The Gaelic festival of Samhain is

   ☐ now a modern Christian holiday.
   ☑ the origin of Halloween.
   ☐ the Celtic name for "harvest".
   ☐ still celebrated in the winter.

🖋 *Hinweis: Bei der entsprechenden Textstelle ist die relevante Information lediglich in umgekehrter Reihenfolge formuliert: "The origin of our modern holiday 'Halloween' goes back to the old Gaelic festival of 'Samhain'" (Z. 1/2) Die anderen Antworten sind inhaltlich falsch.*

b) The celebration of Samhain took

   ☑ about 24 hours.
   ☐ one night.
   ☐ two days.
   ☐ the whole season.

🖋 *Hinweis: Das Fest wurde einen Tag lang – von Sonnenuntergang des 31. Oktober bis Sonnenuntergang des 1. November – gefeiert: "which was celebrated from sunset on October 31st to sunset on November 1st." (Z. 3/4)*

c) It was celebrated

- ☐ only in Scotland.
- ☐ on all of the British islands.
- ✓ at least in Ireland.
- ☐ only in the UK.

*✦ **Hinweis:** Hier muss man die falschen Lösungen ausschließen: Irland, wo „Samhain" früher gefeiert wurde, gehört nicht zum Vereinigten Königreich, und dass es auf allen Britischen Inseln oder nur in Schottland gefeiert wurde, ist als Information nicht im Text enthalten. Darum stimmt nur, dass es zumindest in Irland als Fest gefeiert wurde: "Samhain, which was celebrated in what is now Ireland, the Isle of Man and parts of Scotland" (Z. 7/8)*

d) The "aos sí" are

- ☐ gods of the Irish people.
- ☐ Celts that believed in elves.
- ✓ some kind of fairies.
- ☐ Celts with superpowers.

*✦ **Hinweis:** "the 'aos sí', which is a mystical and supernatural race comparable to fairies or elves" (Z. 9/10)*

e) The Celts believed that the spirits could come into our world

- ☐ only on Midsummer's Eve.
- ✓ whenever they wanted.
- ☐ only on Halloween.
- ☐ only on Samhain.

*✦ **Hinweis:** Hier musst du Z. 11–13 genau lesen. Im Text wird erwähnt, dass an den beiden genannten Feiertagen dem Glauben nach die Geister leichter in unsere Welt kommen konnten. Das bedeutet, dass sie es prinzipiell immer konnten. Zudem schließt die Formulierung „only on" die anderen Antworten aus.*

f) Some chairs at the table were left empty on Samhain

- ✓ because they were for the dead relatives.
- ☐ for the small gifts collected by the people.
- ☐ to turn unpleasant spirits away.
- ☐ only for good and gentle spirits.

*✦ **Hinweis:** "people put empty chairs next to their own, which were meant for the dead members of the family." (Z. 16/17)*
Beachte, dass dabei nicht gesagt wird, dass diese Verwandten gute und wohlmeinende oder unerwünschte Geister sind.

g) If you do not open your door on Halloween,
- ☐ the children do not come to your house.
- ☐ evil spirits do bad things to you.
- ☐ you do not get sweets as a present.
- ☑ some children may play tricks on you.

✦ **Hinweis:** *"the children play tricks on people who do not open the door"* *(Z. 23/24)*

h) Christmas is linked to a
- ☐ Jewish holiday.
- ☑ Roman festival.
- ☐ Gaelic celebration.
- ☐ Celtic tradition.

✦ **Hinweis:** *"The day of the birth of Christ [...] became connected to the Roman 'Festival of the Sun'" (Z. 27/28) Beachte hier, dass das Weihnachtsfest nicht direkt genannt wird; stattdessen ist im Text nur von Christi Geburt die Rede.*

i) "Halloween" is
- ☑ on October 31st.
- ☐ short for "All Hallows' Day".
- ☐ another name for "All Saints' Day".
- ☐ on November 1st.

✦ **Hinweis:** *Lass dich hier nicht von der Langform „All Hallows' Day" verwirren, die lediglich für „Allerheiligen" steht, dem Tag nach „Halloween". Im Text heißt es: "the main date of Samhain – November 1st – turning the night before into 'All Hallows' Evening'. Over the years, decades and centuries, the phrase was shortened to become the word 'Halloween'" (Z. 31–34)*

k) People do not remember the meaning of Halloween because
- ☐ they do not want to be childish.
- ☐ it has no purpose at all.
- ☐ there are no real evil spirits.
- ☑ the original meaning has been lost.

✦ **Hinweis:** *"the meaning behind those rites has been lost over the centuries." (Z. 39/40)*

3. Slam

Hinweis: Lies dir zuerst die Fragen durch, damit du weißt, worauf du beim Lesen achten sollst. Markiere dann beim Lesen die Textstellen, die die Antworten enthalten. Lies immer ganz genau, denn es kann sein, dass es eine Textstelle gibt, die auf den ersten Blick so aussieht, als enthielte sie die Antwort auf eine Frage, obwohl die richtige Antwort eigentlich ein paar Zeilen weiter oben oder unten gegeben wird.

a) He thought they were dead cool.

Hinweis: "at first I thought they were dead cool" (Z. 2)
„they're all right" (Z. 6) ist nicht korrekt, denn dieser Satz drückt aus, was Sam jetzt denkt, es wird aber danach gefragt, was er am Anfang dachte.

b) He teaches literature at a college./He is a (literature) teacher at a college.

Hinweis: "He teaches literature at a college" (Z. 4)

c) – She doesn't understand films/*The Simpsons.*
   – Sam has had to help her with her maths.

Hinweis: "When we went to see films, she didn't understand them, and she never got what anyone was laughing at in The Simpsons, and I had to help her with her maths." (Z. 9–11)
"Her mum and dad helped her with her English." (Z. 11) ist hier nicht richtig, da gefragt ist, warum Sam klüger ist als Alicia. Dass sie in Englisch Hilfe braucht, heißt aber noch nicht, dass Sam in Englisch besser ist als sie.

d) He would like to study art and design at college.

Hinweis: "'He's going to do art and design at college'" (Z. 29)

e) She is working./She likes reading./It is important for her that Sam does his homework./She absolutely wanted to go to college.

Hinweis: "I have […] a mum who's in work and who likes reading and who gets on my case if I haven't done my homework …" (Z. 38/39)/"She was desperate to go to college" (Z. 43/44)

f) Education is not important to him./He thinks education is bad./He thinks education makes you a bad person./

Hinweis: "'Even my dad not being around was a good thing; because he's not into education at all." (Z. 40/41)/"as far as people like my dad are concerned, you're a bad person if you do [read and study]" (Z. 46/47)

g) They think Sam is stupid because he does not have an academic background/because he is not from an educated family.

Hinweis: Aus dem ersten Absatz kannst du herauslesen, dass Alicias Eltern gebildet sind (er unterrichtet Literatur und sie gibt Schauspielunterricht). Zu Sam sagt Andrea "'You haven't had the same advantages as a lot of people.'" (Z. 36/37) und meint damit, dass Sam nicht aus einem akademischen

23

Haushalt kommt. Das ist für Alicias Eltern ein Nachteil; für sie ist weniger Bildung gleichbedeutend mit weniger Intelligenz.

h) For him, being a good person does not depend on education.
Hinweis: *Aus dieser Aussage geht hervor, dass „ein guter Mensch sein" für Sam unabhängig davon ist, wie gebildet jemand ist. Zum Beispiel klingt im Text an, dass Sam es schätzt, dass seine Mutter sich gut um ihn kümmert (vgl. Z. 38–39), auch wenn die Familie keinen akademischen Hintergrund hat. Außerdem findet er es nicht gut, dass Alicias Eltern ihn fälschlicherweise für dumm und Alicia für intelligent halten (vgl. Z. 7–15) und dass sie so tun, als hätte Sam keine guten Chancen für die Zukunft (vgl. Z. 19–26).*

C Use of Language

1. Mediation

Hinweis: *Bei dieser Aufgabe sollst du zwischen einem Hotelangestellten und deinen Freunden dolmetschen. Die Freunde geben dir Informationen oder Fragen vor, die du sinngemäß an einen englischsprachigen Rezeptionisten weitergeben sollst. Anschließend sollst du dessen Antworten und seine Fragen den Freunden auf Deutsch mitteilen. Achte immer genau auf die jeweils geforderte Zielsprache – die eckigen Klammern vor den Antwortzeilen helfen dir dabei. Du sollst hier nicht alles Wort für Wort übersetzen. Manchmal gibt es mehr als eine Möglichkeit, etwas in der Zielsprache auszudrücken.*

ANGESTELLTER:	Good afternoon, how can I help you?
DU:	Good afternoon. We haven't made a reservation. Do you have any rooms for us anyway?
ANGESTELLTER:	Yes, we do. How long would you like to stay?
DU [D]:	**Wie lange wollen wir (hier) bleiben?**
FREUNDE:	Wollten wir nicht eine Woche bleiben und dann weiter an die Küste?
DU [E]:	**We'd like to stay for a week. / We'd like a room for a week.**
ANGESTELLTER:	How many rooms do you need?
DU [D]:	**Wie viele Zimmer brauchen/möchten wir?**
FREUNDE:	Also, Laura und Christian wollen ein Doppelzimmer und Julian schläft sehr unruhig und hätte deswegen gern ein Einzelzimmer. Was ist mit dir und mir? Wir nehmen einfach ein Zimmer mit zwei Einzelbetten.

DU [E]:	**We would like/need a double, a single and a twin room, please.**
ANGESTELLTER:	Would you like to have rooms with bathrooms or rooms with bathrooms in the hall?
DU [D]:	**Wollen wir die Zimmer mit oder ohne Bad? Das Bad wäre sonst ein Gemeinschaftsbad.**
FREUNDE:	Das kommt auf den Preis an. Vielleicht kannst du mal fragen, wie viel die Zimmer kosten?
DU [E]:	**How much are the rooms with and without bathrooms?**
ANGESTELLTER:	The single will be £ 39, the double or the twin room £ 72 a night. With the bathroom in the hall you would pay £ 15 less per room.
DU [D]:	**Das Einzelzimmer kostet 39 £, das Doppelzimmer und das Zweibettzimmer 72 £ die Nacht. Ohne Bad ist das Zimmer um 15 £ billiger.**
FREUNDE:	Dann nehmen wir die Zimmer mit Bad.
DU [E]:	**We'll take the rooms with bathrooms.**
ANGESTELLTER:	Excellent. Could you just fill out these forms for me, please?
DU [D]:	**Wir müssen jetzt noch die Formulare ausfüllen.**
ANGESTELLTER:	Thank you. Here are your room keys. You can use the lift to get to the third floor. Enjoy your stay.

2. Words and structures

Hinweis: In dieser Aufgabe werden deine Kenntnisse in Grammatik und Wortschatz überprüft. Wenn du dir bei einer grammatikalischen Form nicht sicher bist oder die Lücke falsch ausgefüllt hast, lies die entsprechenden Regeln in der Kurzgrammatik (auf der Onlineplattform MyStark) noch einmal nach. Beachte auch, dass drei Wörter aus dem Kasten übrig bleiben.

In the (1) **story** "A Christmas Carol" by Charles Dickens, the reader is (2) **taught** an important lesson. Ebenezer Scrooge, the main character, is a (3) **rich** and nasty old man. He gets to see his past, (4) **present** and future with the help of three ghosts during the night before Christmas and finally realises that he has to (5) **change** his behaviour.

Charles Dickens called the story his "little Christmas book" and it was the novelist's (6) **first** of five Christmas books. "A Christmas Carol" was a great success right (7) **from** the beginning and (8) **over** six thousand copies were sold in one week. Originally written in six weeks by Dickens, who was under financial pressure to pay (9) **off** a debt, the tale has become one of the most (10) **popular** Christmas stories of all time.

Some historians have suggested that the popularity of the tale has actually played a (11) **major** role in shaping the (12) **meaning** of Christmas and the spirit of the holiday.

◢ Hinweise:

zu 1: „A Christmas Carol" wurde von Charles Dickens verfasst. Das einzige vorgegebene Nomen, das ein schriftstellerisches Werk bezeichnet, ist „story".

zu 2: Hier musst du eine Verbform vervollständigen, die mit „is" eingeleitet wird. Achte genau auf die englische Satzkonstruktion; im Deutschen würde der Satz heißen: „Dem Leser wird etw. beigebracht." Die Passivform benötigt hier somit das Partizip „taught".

zu 3: In der Beschreibung des Hauptcharakters fehlt neben „nasty old man" ein weiteres Adjektiv. In den Kontext passt nur „rich".

zu 4: Die Aufzählung von Vergangenheit („past") bis Zukunft („future") lässt nur den Schluss zu, dass die Gegenwart („present") in der Lücke stehen muss.

zu 5: Hier muss auf die Wendung „to have to" (= „müssen") ein Verb im Infinitiv stehen. Der Nebensatz bedeutet im Deutschen: „dass er sein Verhalten (= ‚behaviour') <u>ändern</u> muss."

zu 6: Auf die Lücke folgt die Wendung „of five Christmas books". Das sollte dir den entscheidenden Hinweis geben, dass es sich um eine Reihung handelt: „die <u>erste</u> von fünf Weihnachtsgeschichten".

zu 7: Hier fehlt ein Wort aus der zusammenhängenden Wendung „right <u>from</u> the beginning" (= „von Anfang an"). Präge dir diese Formulierung gut ein.

zu 8: Wenn du den Kontext genau beachtest, wirst du feststellen, dass nur die Option „over" infrage kommt, denn es wurden „über 6 000 Exemplare verkauft".

zu 9: Das deutsche Verb „abbezahlen" wird im Englischen mit „to pay <u>off</u>" wiedergegeben.

zu 10: Die Steigerungsform eines Adjektivs wird hier mit „most" eingeleitet. Von den angegebenen Adjektiven passt nur „popular" in den Kontext.

zu 11: Hier fehlt ein Adjektiv, das sich auf „role" bezieht. Der Ausdruck „eine große Rolle spielen" wird im Englischen mit „to play a <u>major</u> role" wiedergegeben. Du solltest dir diesen Ausdruck gut einprägen.

zu 12: Sowohl der Artikel „the" vor der Lücke, als auch der Ausdruck „of Christmas" danach, lassen auf ein fehlendes Nomen schließen. Beachte, dass „Meinung" (= „opinion") und „meaning" (= „Bedeutung") so genannte „false friends" sind. In diesem Fall passt nur „meaning" in die Lücke.

D Text Production

Hinweis: In der Textproduktion kannst du zwischen zwei Themen wählen. Lies zuerst beide Themen aufmerksam durch und überlege genau, welches dir mehr liegt. Insgesamt sollst du einen Text von rund 150 Wörtern verfassen. Achte beim Schreiben darauf, dass du die Vorgaben der Aufgabenstellung berücksichtigst. Lies am Ende noch einmal deinen ganzen Text konzentriert durch. Korrigiere dabei Grammatik- und Rechtschreibfehler. Überprüfe auch, ob dein Text logisch aufgebaut ist. Die Beispiellösungen sind etwas länger als die geforderten 150 Wörter, da hier auf alle Aspekte eingegangen wird. Du brauchst in deiner Antwort aber nur auf vier der fünf Fragen antworten.

Tell the story behind the picture.

Last year my family and I travelled to the UK for the holidays. We visited the beautiful county of Kent in the southeast of England, where you can find lots of old English churches. I took a very nice picture of a church and the surrounding buildings. When we were home again, my mom asked me to print the picture in poster size to give it to my dad as a present for his birthday. He should be able to remember our fantastic trip. I sent the picture to a photo company, but when I got the poster, I was shocked. There was a white spot on the right-hand side of the picture just below the church. It did not look like a printing error. What could it be? Suddenly I remembered: On that day our tour guide had told us a story about a famous white gravestone that had once been in front of the church. The stone had disappeared one day and nobody has been able to find it again. Maybe the ghost of the dead person was still there and could only be seen on photographs?

However, three days later, the photo company sent an email to apologise for the bad picture quality. So there was no ghost after all.   *213 words*

Dear Diary …

Dear Diary,

We are back – finally! Those last two weeks on holiday were the most awful two weeks of my whole life. At first, when my parents told me that we would be travelling to the US to drive the famous Route 66 in a big motor caravan together, I was pretty excited. We flew from Frankfurt to Chicago and fetched our "camper", which looked quite nice, but after our first day on tour, the vehicle broke down and we had to phone the company to get a replacement. As they did not have another motor caravan, we got a normal car which did not even have enough space for all our things. Understandably, I was quite annoyed. For the rest of our trip we had to find hotel rooms for every single night, which meant that we sometimes had to spend our nights in cheap road motels. Once, I found three cockroaches and two big spiders in one night. That was really, really disgusting! But the worst thing happened when we drove through Albuquerque, New Mexico: First, our car was stopped by the police for inspection and then, the policemen turned out to be robbers that took all of our money, my parents' credit cards and my new smartphone. It was absolutely terrible! So I am really glad that the trip is finally over! *225 words*

A Listening Comprehension

Hinweis: Der „Listening Comprehension Test" besteht aus drei Teilen. Den beiden Nachrichtenmeldungen in Teil 1 und den Interviews in Teil 2 und 3 sind jeweils „Listening Tasks" zugeordnet, die in Abschlussprüfungen häufig vorkommen. Bevor du die einzelnen Texte hörst, hast du Zeit, dich mit der jeweiligen Aufgabenstellung vertraut zu machen.

Part One

Hinweis: Zu jeder Nachrichtenmeldung werden dir vier Satzanfänge mit drei möglichen Satzenden vorgegeben. Deine Aufgabe ist es, das jeweils richtige Satzende zu finden. Lies dir die Satzanfänge und Wahlmöglichkeiten genau durch, damit du beim Hören weißt, worauf du achten musst. Beachte, dass auch die falschen Satzenden im Text in einem anderen Zusammenhang vorkommen können.

News Item 1

a) Orion's first flight took place
- [✓] on December 5th.
- [ ] on a Friday in November.
- [ ] on a Thursday morning.

Hinweis: "NASA's Orion space programme has finally begun. On Friday, 5 December, a rocket carrying the new spacecraft started off ..." (Z. 1–3)

b) NASA's plan is to send people to Mars in
- [ ] the 2020s.
- [ ] 40 years.
- [✓] the 2030s.

Hinweis: "The new Orion spacecraft is able to get up to six people [...] to Mars by the middle of the 2030s." (Z. 9–13)

c) The flight test lasted for
- [ ] less than 4 hours.
- [✓] 4 ½ hours.
- [ ] more than 4 ½ hours.

Hinweis: "the trip didn't last longer than four and a half hours." (Z. 14/15)

d) The capsule finally landed
- [ ] at Cape Canaveral.
- [x] in the sea.
- [ ] on a Navy ship.

Hinweis: *"After the capsule had landed safely in the Pacific Ocean ..."* (Z. 17/18)

News Item 2

a) The casting show "The Voice" was originally
- [ ] British.
- [x] Dutch.
- [ ] Chinese.

Hinweis: *"the casting show was first aired in the Netherlands"* (Z. 4/5)

b) In Italy,
- [ ] a 52-year-old nun won this year's series.
- [ ] Alicia Keys sang a love song in the final.
- [x] Sister Cristina performed the song "No One".

Hinweis: *"25-year-old nun Cristina Scuccia won 'The Voice of Italy' by singing Alicia Keys' love song 'No One'."* (Z. 10–12)

c) Cristina Scuccia's reason to participate in the casting show was
- [ ] to persuade others to become Christian.
- [ ] to earn money for her church.
- [x] to share God's love with the audience.

Hinweis: *"her reason for performing was to spread the message of God's love and not to earn money"* (Z. 18–20)

d) Cristina's performance reached
- [ ] mainly the Italian television viewers.
- [x] a worldwide audience.
- [ ] especially young people on YouTube.

Hinweis: *"Cristina's winning performance also earned her a record number of clicks on YouTube throughout the world."* (Z. 23–25); die dritte Möglichkeit ist hier nicht richtig, da Cristina nicht nur junge Leute auf YouTube erreicht.

Part Two

Hinweis: In diesem Hörtext werden sieben Passanten zum Thema Urlaub befragt. Anhand ihrer Äußerungen musst du die Gedankenblasen A–H den richtigen Personen zuordnen und in die Tabelle eintragen. Eine Gedankenblase bleibt bei dieser Matching-Aufgabe übrig.

John	Olivia	Hailey	Carter	Josh	Sara	Lara
H	C	E	G	F	A	D

Hinweise:

zu John: "my wife and I usually go to a luxurious boutique hotel on Vancouver Island that doesn't allow small children. We go for long walks in the woods, get massages, go to the sauna and enjoy the fantastic food there." (Z. 10–15)

zu Olivia: "I don't want to be seen as a tourist […]. I usually go couchsurfing […]. It's a great and cheap way to meet locals, make new friends and explore places far away from the typical tourist paths." (Z. 18–23)

zu Hailey: "I wouldn't like to go couchsurfing. I think it's dangerous" (Z. 24–26)

zu Carter: "I love hiking and fishing and being outside 24/7" (Z. 34/35)

zu Josh: "Camping is great, isn't it?" (Z. 39); "I like sleeping in the comfy bed of the mobile home" (Z. 41–43)

zu Sara: "Staying at a hotel's just too expensive" (Z. 49/50)

zu Lara: "my best friend Lisa still lives in Frankfurt, so when I go on holiday, I always visit her." (Z. 56–58)

Part Three

Hinweis: Deine Aufgabe ist es, die Tabelle mit den fehlenden Informationen in Stichpunkten zu vervollständigen. Lies die Aufgabenstellung genau und halte dich an die Vorgaben; so ist es z. B. bei „one reason why she enjoys working on set" ausreichend, nur einen Aspekt zu nennen. Bei „nationalities of Jennifer's great-grandparents" zeigt dir der Plural, dass du zwei Informationen einfügen musst.

(1) the year Jennifer Brown was born	**1979**
(2) nationalities of Jennifer's great-grandparents	**German, English**
(3) the period of time she worked in San Francisco	**5 years / five years**
(4) the reason why Jennifer dropped out of university	**to work (just) as an actress / started working as an actress**

31

(5) one reason why she enjoys working on set	they have lots of fun on set / everyone works really hard / everybody is supportive and respectful / she can be herself / she can be creative
(6) the reason why Jennifer likes Shakespeare plays	he uses wonderful words
(7) how people react when they see Jennifer on the street (one aspect)	they stare / a lot of people stare / they tell her that she looks familiar / they ask her, "Do I know you"? / they ask her whether they know her
(8) her hobbies (two examples)	writing scripts / reading plays / training her dogs / training her two German Shepherds / hiking / skiing
(9) a foreign language she speaks okay	French
(10) a German city Jennifer would like to visit	(the) capital (city) / Berlin

Hinweise:

zu 1: "I was born in Vancouver in 1979." (Z. 5/6)

zu 2: "my great-grandparents were from England and Germany." (Z. 6–8)
Beachte, dass hier nach den Nationalitäten, und nicht nach den Herkunftsländern der Urgroßeltern gefragt wird. Du musst also die Adjektive zu den im Text genannten Ländernamen bilden.

zu 3: "I worked in a hotel in San Francisco for five years" (Z. 10/11)

zu 4: "I got into acting as a way to pay for my tuition, but later I gave up my studies to work just as an actress. Now, I couldn't imagine doing anything else." (Z. 14–17)

zu 5: "I don't think I can put into words how much fun we usually have on set. Everyone works really hard and they're totally supportive and respectful. I always feel like I can be myself. It's great to be creative." (Z. 21–25)

zu 6: "He uses wonderful words." (Z. 35)

zu 7: "A lot of people just stare, or tell me that I look familiar. And I get 'Do I know you?' a lot." (Z. 38–40)

zu 8: Hier musst du zwei Hobbys erwähnen, um den Punkt zu erhalten: "What are your hobbies? – Writing scripts, reading plays and training my two German Shepherds. I also love hiking and skiing, but I hardly ever find the time." (Z. 51–55)

zu 9: Hier ist „French" die einzige richtige Lösung. Zwar verwendet Jennifer deutsche Befehle für ihre Hunde, aber ansonsten spricht sie die Sprache nicht: "I can get by nicely with my French." (Z. 58/59)

zu 10: "I've never been to Berlin. I'd love to see the capital of Germany." (Z. 67/68)

B Reading Comprehension

Hinweis: Im Prüfungsteil Leseverstehen begegnen dir bisweilen recht anspruchsvolle Texte. Lass dich vom Umfang und sprachlichen Niveau dieser Texte nicht verunsichern, da du oftmals nicht jedes einzelne Wort verstehen musst, um die gestellten Aufgaben zu beantworten. Lies dir die Aufgaben aber immer gut durch, da hier meist mehr Details als in den Hörverstehensaufgaben gefordert werden. Dafür hast du aber auch die Möglichkeit, dir die Texte mehrmals genau durchzulesen.

1. Canada Facts and Figures

Hinweis: Bei dieser Aufgabe sollst du den einzelnen Abschnitten (1–5) des Lesetextes über Kanada passende Überschriften (A–G) zuordnen. Sieh dir vor dem ersten Lesen des Textes die möglichen Überschriften an. Beim Lesen des Textes ist es sinnvoll, Schlüsselwörter zu unterstreichen oder hervorzuheben. So kannst du dich im Anschluss leichter für die jeweils am besten passende Überschrift entscheiden. Denke daran, dass die Überschriften sich jeweils auf den gesamten Absatz beziehen müssen und nicht nur Teilaspekte abdecken. Zwei „headings" bleiben übrig.

part of the text	❶	❷	❸	❹	❺
heading	C	D	E	G	B

Hinweise:

zu 1: Der erste Absatz beschäftigt sich mit der Geographie Kanadas. Schlüsselwörter, die dir zeigen, dass „C" die richtige Überschrift sein muss, sind z. B. „ten provinces"; „three territories"; „largest territory is Nunavut in the far north"; „the Pacific Ocean in the west, the Atlantic Ocean in the east and the Arctic Ocean in the North".

zu 2: Der zweite Absatz handelt von Nunavut. Auf den ersten Blick könntest du geneigt sein, diesem Textteil Überschrift „F" (Winter in Nunavut) zuzuordnen. Wenn du allerdings genau liest, stellst du fest, dass diese Überschrift nur einen Teil des Abschnittes abdeckt. In dem Abschnitt erfahren wir z. B. darüber hinaus, welchen täglichen Herausforderungen sich die Bewohner dieses ganz im Norden *gelegenen „territory" stellen müssen: „there are no roads that connect the 25 communities". Daher ist „D" die richtige Lösung.*

zu 3: *Auch bei diesem Absatz musst du aufpassen, da auf den ersten Blick die beiden Überschriften „A" und „E" infrage kommen könnten. Allerdings handelt dieser Textabschnitt nur von den beiden Amtssprachen Englisch und Franzö- sisch. Dass Kanada multilingual ist und viele weitere Sprachen in Gebrauch sind, wird hier nicht erwähnt. Daher ist „E" die richtige Überschrift.*

zu 4: *In diesem Abschnitt geht es um die kanadischen Nationalparks. Es werden sowohl die Geschichte, die Anzahl und Größe der Parks sowie die möglichen Akti- vitäten in den Parks angesprochen. Hier musst du also Überschrift „G" angeben.*

zu 5: *Der letzte Abschnitt beschäftigt sich mit einem beliebten Touristenziel, den Niagarafällen. Es wird beschrieben, welche Möglichkeiten Besuchern geboten werden, die Wasserfälle zu erleben: "One way to experience the falls is to go on a breathtaking 'Journey Behind the Falls'"; "Thrill-seeking visitors, however, might want to go on a cruise"; "the American side is also worth a visit." Hier passt also Überschrift „B".*

2. Vancouver, B.C.

*✏ **Hinweis:** Hier hast du vier Auswahlmöglichkeiten und musst für die Satzan- fänge die jeweils passende Satzergänzung finden. Lies die Optionen ganz genau durch, da manchmal nur ein Wort entscheidend sein kann.*

a) Vancouver

  ☐ is a city in Britain.
  ☑ is a city in North America.
  ☐ is located 50 miles away from the American border.
  ☐ has 630,000 inhabitants.

*✏ **Hinweis:** "Vancouver is a beautiful city with <u>more than</u> 630,000 inhabitants on the <u>west coast of Canada</u>, about 50 <u>kilometres</u> away from the border to the United States" (Z. 1/2)*

b) The Rocky Mountains are

  ☑ near Vancouver.
  ☐ a long way from Vancouver.
  ☐ in Vancouver.
  ☐ surrounded by water.

*✏ **Hinweis:** "Vancouver [...] is <u>close to</u> the Rocky Mountains." (Z. 5/6)*

c) Vancouver

- [✓] is not the capital of British Columbia.
- [ ] is the capital city of British Columbia.
- [ ] is the capital of Quebec.
- [ ] is the capital of Ontario.

Hinweis: "*Vancouver is situated in the province of British Columbia, which is the third-largest province after Quebec and Ontario. The <u>capital city</u> of this province is <u>not Vancouver</u> but Victoria.*" *(Z. 7–9)*

d) In 2010, Vancouver

- [ ] had a record number of visitors.
- [ ] became the most popular tourist destination in Canada.
- [ ] was the rainiest place in Canada.
- [✓] organized the Olympic and Paralympic Games.

Hinweis: Vor einigen Jahren war Vancouver Gastgeber der Olympischen Spiele: "*In 2010, the city of Vancouver <u>hosted</u> the Olympic and Paralympic Winter Games.*" *(Z. 10)*

e) Stanley Park

- [ ] is the largest inner-city park in North America.
- [✓] has many attractions for children and adults alike.
- [ ] is located close to Kitsilano.
- [ ] is located on the outskirts of Vancouver.

Hinweis: "*Stanley Park, which is located on a peninsula in the heart of Vancouver, is one of the largest inner-city parks in North America and definitely worth a visit, with many <u>attractions for the entire family</u> on offer.*" *(Z. 13–16)*

f) Gastown

- [ ] is great for doing sports.
- [ ] is fantastic for going shopping.
- [✓] is the birthplace of Vancouver.
- [ ] is famous for its clock powered by electricity.

Hinweis: "*Gastown, the city's <u>original settlement</u> …*" *(Z. 18/19)*

g) Vancouver

- [ ] is the greenest city in the world.
- [ ] has got 150,000 trees.
- [✓] city authorities fine people for smoking in public.
- [ ] is the cleanest city in Canada.

Hinweis: "*Vancouver is a very clean city […] maybe because city <u>authorities issue tickets for smoking</u>, spitting or peeing in public places.*" *(Z. 21/22)*

35

h) In Vancouver,
- ☐ the public transport system is excellent.
- ☑ the quality of life is excellent.
- ☐ most people can afford to buy a house.
- ☐ most people walk or cycle to work.

Hinweis: "The quality of life in Vancouver is said to be one of the best in the world." (Z. 28)

i) ____ of the city's inhabitants speak English as their mother tongue.
- ☐ 35 %
- ☑ 48 %
- ☐ 52 %
- ☐ 65 %

Hinweis: Wenn 52 % der Bewohner eine andere Muttersprache als Englisch sprechen, sind 48 % „native speakers of English": "52 % of the city's inhabitants do not speak English as their first language." (Z. 30/31)

k) ____ were very important for the economy of the city thirty years ago.
- ☐ The film industry and fishing
- ☐ Forestry and tourism
- ☐ Software development and agriculture
- ☑ Forestry and mining

Hinweis: "Thirty years ago, the city's economy relied mainly on forestry, mining, fishing and agriculture." (Z. 35/36)

3. An email from Vancouver

Hinweis: Zu dieser E-Mail musst du Fragen beantworten. Lies dir zuerst die Fragen durch, damit du weißt, worauf du beim Lesen achten sollst. Markiere dann beim Lesen die entsprechenden Textstellen. Du darfst die Formulierungen aus dem Text direkt übernehmen. Unbekannte Wörter, die du in deiner Antwort verwendest, solltest du aber unbedingt immer vorher nachschlagen.

a) He has just moved to Vancouver / Canada.

Hinweis: "How are you and how is life back in England? I miss you guys a lot, but I'm slowly getting used to life in Vancouver."

b) The films that were produced there, are, for example "The Twilight Saga" / "Juno" or "Night at the Museum".

Hinweis: "Did you know, for example, that Vancouver's often called 'Hollywood North' because many films and TV series are produced here? I know that you have seen 'The Twilight Saga', 'Juno' and 'Night at the Museum'. They were all (partly) made in and around Vancouver!"

c) Film-making in Vancouver is accessible because there are no high walls, whereas in the United States film productions are walled off.

Hinweis: "Vancouver's bustling with actors and film productions. I think it's very different from L.A., though. There aren't any high walls, but film-making here is accessible"

d) You might run into the shooting of a film, especially in the summer months, but you have to be lucky. / Finding a film-shooting is like finding a needle in a haystack.

Hinweis: "But don't think you'll see a film crew on every corner. It's more like finding a needle in a haystack."

e) You have to walk along the streets with your eyes open and be able to interpret the signs. Red arrows or big white trucks with "mobile dressing room" or "location caterer" printed on them show you that a film is being shot nearby.

Hinweis: "You have to keep your eyes open and be able to interpret the signs. [...] My classmates have told me that if I see a red arrow, I'm on the right track. Or that I should look for big white trucks with the words 'mobile dressing rooms' or 'location caterers' written on the side."

f) While buying an ice cream in a store a woman saw Mel Gibson. She put her ice cream in her handbag to ask him for an autograph.

Hinweis: "the woman [...] saw Mel Gibson coming in. She was so excited that she put her ice cream in her handbag to ask him for an autograph."

g) The film crew put rubbish on this street before a film shooting, and then went for lunch. When they returned from lunch, the street cleaners had cleaned the street up again.

Hinweis: "the story of an American film team that needed a small but dirty street for a film-shooting, so they put rubbish on this street. After they had finished preparing the street, they went for lunch. When they returned, the street cleaners had cleaned the street up again ..."

h) The actor likes the city, because there is lots of water (around it). / ... its inhabitants are calm. / ... people feel quite safe there.

Hinweis: "He once said in an interview that he liked the city because of the relationship to the water and the calmness of the people. He also added that there was less fear there."

C Use of Language

1. Mediation

Hinweis: Denke daran, dass du hier keine wörtliche Übersetzung anfertigen sollst. Du musst dem Flyer die entsprechenden Informationen entnehmen und sie im ersten Teil der Aufgabe (a–f) ins Deutsche übertragen. Im zweiten Teil (g–l) musst du vorgegebene deutsche Sätze auf Englisch in Frageform formulieren.

a) in North Vancouver / nur 10 Minuten von der Innenstadt (entfernt)
   Hinweis: "*Just ten minutes from the heart of downtown is […] Capilano Suspension Bridge, located in North Vancouver.*"

b) im Zentrum von Vancouver / im Stadtzentrum
   Hinweis: "*Our tours start in the heart of Vancouver.*"

c) 137 m lang und 70 m hoch
   Hinweis: "*It is one of the longest, highest and most spectacular suspended footbridges in the world, spanning 137 metres across the Capilano River canyon at a height of 70 metres.*"

d) (im Jahr) 2011
   Hinweis: "*the Cliffwalk, the newest addition to the park opened in 2011.*"

e) dort gibt es die Möglichkeit, tolle/beeindruckende Fotos zu machen
   Hinweis: "*Cleveland Dam, where there's an impressive photo opportunity.*"

f) (man hat einen atemberaubenden Blick über) die Stadt, das Meer und die umliegenden Berge
   Hinweis: "*We take […] the famous 'Skyride' gondola to enjoy breathtaking views of the city, the ocean and the surrounding mountains.*"

g) Does the tour take place every day? / Is it possible to take the tour daily?

h) What time / When does the tour start?

i) How long does the tour last? / How long is the tour?

k) Is there also a stop in Chinatown (during the tour)? / Does the tour stop in Chinatown too?
   Hinweis: In Entscheidungsfragen, die mit „Ja" oder „Nein" beantwortet werden, steht das (erste) Hilfsverb immer am Anfang.

l) How much is a (single) ticket for an adult and are there any reduced prices for students? / How much does the tour cost for an adult and is there a student discount? / How much are adult tickets and are there special prices for students?

2. Words and structures

*✎ **Hinweis:** In dieser Aufgabe werden deine Kenntnisse in Grammatik und Wortschatz mithilfe eines Lückentextes überprüft. Du musst aus den vorgegebenen Wörtern im Kasten das jeweils richtige heraussuchen und in die entsprechende Lücke setzen. Betrachte die Satzstruktur und den Kontext genau, um Wörter auszuschließen. Vier Wörter können gar nicht verwendet werden. Während du die Aufgabe bearbeitest, streiche die von dir verwendeten Wörter im Kasten mit Bleistift durch; überprüfe deine Wahl aber auch im weiteren Verlauf der Aufgabe immer wieder, um sicherzustellen, dass du sie für die richtige Lücke verwendet hast. Wenn du unsicher bist oder eine Lücke falsch ausgefüllt hast, lies die entsprechenden Regeln in der Kurzgrammatik (auf der Onlineplattform MyStark) noch einmal nach.*

For (1) **many** years now, history teacher Mary Green from Vancouver High School (2) **has taken** a group of high school students to Europe. (3) **Each** year, it has been an adventure for both her and the students. The past spring was no different. They (4) **visited** Scotland first, then drove through the English (5) **countryside** and crossed the English Channel to France to go to Paris. Each area was very (6) **different** from the others and each held its own charm.

In Scotland the group landed at Glasgow Airport and (7) **went** to Edinburgh immediately. After a short stay, they stopped briefly at Gretna Green, then drove into England, spent the night in Coventry and reached London the next morning. (8) **After** visiting London, they finally (9) **took** the Eurostar train to Paris, going underneath the English Channel. That was (10) **where** the trip ended. They left from Charles De Gaulle International Airport in the late afternoon on the tenth day.

Every place that they stopped at was a new adventure, (11) **which** was different for each person. Some loved Edinburgh best; (12) **others** preferred London. Most loved the (13) **history** of Paris. And they all learned this: to appreciate places (14) **outside** Canada.

*✎ **Hinweise:***

***zu 1:** Hier fehlt ein Begleiter für das Nomen „years". Der Plural zeigt dir, dass es sich um „mehrere" oder „viele" Jahre handeln muss; von den angegebenen Wörtern passt daher nur „many".*

***zu 2:** Der Ausdruck „for [many] years" ist ein eindeutiges Signal für das „present perfect"; von den beiden möglichen Verbformen macht hier nur „has taken" Sinn, denn Mary Green hat die Schüler nach Europa gebracht.*

***zu 3:** Du solltest hier erkennen, dass das Nomen „year" einen Begleiter benötigt; „each year" bedeutet „jedes Jahr".*

zu 4: *Hier fehlt ein Verb. Wenn du den ganzen Satz liest, erkennst du, dass das Verb im „simple past" stehen muss. Von den angegebenen Verben kommt nur „visited" infrage, da „went" hier ohne die Präposition „to" nicht verwendet werden kann.*

zu 5: *Das Wort „English" ist hier ein Adjektiv und bezieht sich auf ein Nomen. Die Nomen „beach" und „history" passen inhaltlich nicht – daher ist „country-side" die richtige Lösung.*

zu 6: *Die Satzkonstruktion mit dem Adverb „very" zeigt dir, dass hier ein Adjektiv fehlt, auf das die Präposition „from" folgt. Deshalb kommt hier nur „different" infrage.*

zu 7: *Der erste Teil des Satzes gibt die Zeitform vor: Das Verb „landed" steht im „simple past". Da es sich um aufeinanderfolgende Handlungen in der Vergangenheit handelt, muss auch im zweiten Teil des Satzes „simple past" verwendet werden. Die anschließende Richtungsangabe („to Edinburgh") weist auf ein Verb der Bewegung hin. Das gesuchte Wort ist also „went".*

zu 8: *Es handelt sich hier um eine Konstruktion mit dem Partizip „visiting". Da im folgenden Hauptsatz die Zugfahrt nach Paris im Vordergrund steht, muss der Besuch Londons zeitlich vorher stattgefunden haben. Die Konjunktion „after" (= „nachdem") bringt den Zusammenhang in die richtige zeitliche Reihenfolge.*

zu 9: *Die Wendung „den Zug nehmen" hat im Englischen die Entsprechung „to take the train". Das fehlende Verb kann nur im „simple past" stehen, da sie erst London besichtigten und danach mit dem Zug fuhren.*

zu 10: *Im vorhergehenden Satz kommen sie nach Paris – die letzte Station ihrer Reise. Es war „der Ort, <u>an dem</u> ihre Reise endete".*

zu 11: *Die Lücke liegt hier am Anfang eines Relativsatzes, der das Nomen „adventure" näher beschreibt. Es fehlt somit das passende Relativpronomen. Da „adventure" keine Person ist, musst du „which" verwenden.*

zu 12: *Zunächst heißt es, dass „einige Edinburgh am meisten mochten". „Andere" (= „others") mochten hingegen London lieber.*

zu 13: *In diese Lücke gehört ein Nomen. Da Paris keinen Strand hat, bleibt nur „history" als richtige Lösung übrig.*

zu 14: *Sie schätzen Orte „außerhalb Kanadas". Dementsprechend musst du hier „outside" einsetzen.*

D Text Production

*✦ **Hinweis:** In der Textproduktion kannst du zwischen zwei Themen wählen. Lies zuerst beide Themen aufmerksam durch und überlege genau, welches dir mehr liegt. Insgesamt sollst du einen Text von rund 150 Wörtern verfassen. Achte beim Schreiben darauf, dass du alle Vorgaben der Aufgabenstellung berücksichtigst. Lies am Ende noch einmal deinen ganzen Text konzentriert durch. Korrigiere dabei Grammatik- und Wortschatzfehler. Überprüfe auch, ob du einen zusammenhängenden Text geschrieben und alle geforderten Punkte behandelt hast.*

Applying for a job

Dear Sir / Madam,

Referring to the job offer I found in last month's issue of "Cinematic World Magazine", I would like to introduce myself. My name is Steffie Finke and I am very interested in working at your cinema. I am 17 years old, I come from Germany and I love films. Last year, during the summer break, I worked at a big cinema in my home town for three weeks. I sold tickets and worked as an usher. Therefore, I am already experienced in these areas, but I would also be happy to work in the restaurant. I speak English fluently, too.

This coming July, I will be staying in Canada for one year. I am looking for an exciting job in a young team with flexible hours.

Could you please give me more detailed information about what students have to do?

It would be great if you could answer my question. You can reach me by phone or email. I am looking forward to hearing from you.

Yours faithfully,

Steffie Finke
email: steffie@finke.com
phone: 0049 / 69 987 654

172 words

Writing competition: "Your favourite film"

Hinweis: *In dieser Schreibaufgabe sollst du den Inhalt des Films beschreiben und auf drei weitere Aspekte eingehen. In der Angabe werden dir jedoch vier mögliche Aspekte vorgeschlagen. Da in dem folgenden Lösungsvorschlag auf alle vier Fragen eingegangen wird, ist der Text etwas länger als die in der Prüfung geforderte Textlänge.*

There are so many films I really like, but the first film of "The Hunger Games" trilogy is my favourite. I had read the book before watching the film and although I knew what was going to happen, I was still very keen to see how they had adapted the story for the big screen. What I especially like about the film is that a brave girl plays the main role.

The film is set in the future in a state called "Panem", which is divided into twelve districts. Every year, the so-called "Hunger Games" take place, in which two children of each district have to fight against each other until only one of them survives.

I saw the film three times at our local cinema, and I have got the DVD at home, so whenever I feel like it, I watch it again. Jennifer Lawrence, who plays the role of Katniss Everdeen, is a fantastic actress.

In Germany, the film can legally be watched by children who are at least twelve years old. However, I would not want my thirteen-year-old brother to see it. Although most of the violent action is off-screen, the viewers still know what is going on …

202 words

A Listening Comprehension

Hinweis: Im ersten Teil der Abschlussprüfung wird dein Hörverstehen geprüft. Die „Listening Comprehension" besteht aus drei Teilen. Den beiden Durchsagen in Teil 1 und den Interviews in Teil 2 und 3 sind jeweils „Listening Tasks" zugeordnet, die in Abschlussprüfungen häufig vorkommen. Bevor du die einzelnen Texte hörst, hast du Zeit, die entsprechenden Aufgabenstellungen durchzulesen.

Part One

Hinweis: Zu jeder Durchsage werden dir vier Satzanfänge mit drei möglichen Satzenden vorgegeben. Deine Aufgabe ist es, das jeweils richtige Satzende zu finden. Lies dir die Satzanfänge und Wahlmöglichkeiten genau durch, damit du beim Hören weißt, worauf du achten musst. Beachte, dass auch die falschen Satzenden im Text in einem anderen Zusammenhang vorkommen können.

Announcement 1

a) The announcement was made
- ☐ on board Flight PA 7374.
- ☐ on a flight to London Heathrow.
- ☑ on board Flight BA 7374.

Hinweis: "welcome on board Flight BA 7374 from London Heathrow to Singapore." (Z. 1–3)

b) The person speaking is
- ☑ the purser.
- ☐ the co-pilot.
- ☐ the pilot.

Hinweis: "My name is Zoe Anderson and I'm the purser of this flight." (Z. 3/4) Der „Purser" ist der/die ranghöchste Flugbegleiter/in eines Passagierflugzeugs.

c) The plane will land in Singapore at about
- ☑ 11.45 a.m.
- ☐ 10.30 p.m.
- ☐ 2.30 p.m.

Hinweis: "Our estimated time of arrival at Singapore Changi Airport is tomorrow at 11.45 a.m. local time." (Z. 12–14)

d) There will be … in Singapore.

☐ clear skies

☐ a lot of heavy rain

☑ sun and rain

✏ *Hinweis: "The weather in Singapore will be partly <u>sunny with</u> isolated <u>showers</u>." (Z. 18/19)*

Announcement 2

a) The announcement was made on

☑ December 24th.

☐ December 25th.

☐ December 26th.

✏ *Hinweis: "It's Christmas Eve …" (Z. 1)*

b) There will be difficult road conditions

☑ in the South of England.

☐ on Boxing Day only.

☐ according to the Met Office.

✏ *Hinweis: "if you are planning to drive tomorrow, on 25th, and the day after tomorrow, on Boxing Day, <u>in Southern England</u>, make sure you check the weather forecast and road conditions before you hit the road." (Z. 4–8)*
Die Straßenverhältnisse werden sowohl am 25. als auch am 26. Dezember in Südengland schlecht sein. Das „Met Office" (Wetteramt) ist nur für die Wettervorhersage zuständig. Mit der Straßenlage hat es nichts zu tun.

c) All road users

☐ are in danger of being blown over.

☑ have to expect longer travel times.

☐ should travel by caravan or bus.

✏ *Hinweis: "all motorists are advised to allow plenty of extra time" (Z. 16/17)*

d) It is possible to get details on weather conditions by

☑ calling the BBC hotline.

☐ going to the website of the Highways Agency.

☐ turning on the TV.

✏ *Hinweis: "For information on weather conditions […] listen to BBC Radio 2 or phone our hotline on 0300 244 6000." (Z. 21–24)*

Part Two

Hinweis: In diesem Hörtext werden sieben Passanten zum Thema Ernährung befragt. Anhand ihrer Äußerungen musst du die Gedankenblasen A–H den richtigen Personen zuordnen und in die Tabelle eintragen. Eine Gedankenblase bleibt bei dieser Matching-Aufgabe übrig.

Henry	Liam	Clare	Finn	Colin	Hanna	Tessa
D	C	A	F	E	H	B

Hinweise:

zu Henry: *"I'm single and I think it's too much work to cook just for myself"* (Z. 11/12)

zu Liam: *"my freezer's full of ready-made meals, which I simply pop into the microwave."* (Z. 19/20)

zu Clare: *"I've been a vegan for two years. My diet is plant-based and I avoid all animal foods"* (Z. 26–28)

zu Finn: *"There's nothing I enjoy more than a big chunk of steak. All my family love meat"* (Z. 33–35); *"In the summer, we have a barbecue at least once a week."* (Z. 38/39)

zu Colin: *"I got involved in a community garden last year. We share a garden and grow all kinds of fruit and vegetables"* (Z. 44–47)

zu Hanna: *"I consider myself a 'part-time vegetarian', because I usually eat vegetarian meals, but when I go out for dinner, I sometimes order fish or chicken."* (Z. 54–58)

zu Tessa: *"One of my new year resolutions is to lose some weight. That's why I'm trying to cut down on sugar"* (Z. 59–61)

Part Three

Hinweis: Deine Aufgabe ist es, die folgende Tabelle mit den fehlenden Informationen in Stichpunkten zu vervollständigen. Lies die Aufgabenstellung genau und halte dich an die Vorgaben. Ist nur „one example" verlangt, so solltest du auch nur ein Beispiel angeben.

(1) the day the interview takes place	**Tuesday (afternoon)**
(2) the country Amy is in when doing the interview	**Australia**
(3) number of countries where Amy's album is in the charts	**31 / thirty-one**

45

(4) number of copies of "My soul, my life" sold in the UK	(over/more than) 150,000 (copies)
(5) one topic Amy sings about	feeling lonely / feeling angry / feeling insecure / heartbreak / being bullied / moving to a new city
(6) number of cities in Europe where concerts will take place	6 / six
(7) Amy's plans after her European tour	(to) marry / (to) get married / (to) marry her fiancé
(8) reason why Amy's fiancé is able to travel with her	he gave up his job / he quit his job
(9) where Amy sang with the school band (one example)	(at) her school / (at) weddings / (at) (large) birthday parties
(10) reason why Amy is in a hurry	she has a plane to catch / she has to get to the airport / has to catch a plane

Hinweise:

zu 1: "It's two minutes to two on this beautiful Tuesday afternoon." (Z. 1/2)

zu 2: "She is now with us live from Sydney." (Z. 4/5)

zu 3: "Your latest album 'My soul, my life' is high up in the charts in 31 countries" (Z. 8/9)

zu 4: "and has sold over 150,000 copies in the UK alone." (Z. 9/10)

zu 5: "When I sing a song, I tell authentic stories – stories that many teenagers can relate to, such as feeling lonely, angry or insecure. I sing about heartbreak, being bullied or moving to a new city." (Z. 12–16)

zu 6: "There'll be six concerts in Europe's capitals: London, Paris, Madrid, Berlin, Vienna and Rome." (Z. 31–33)

zu 7: "So can we expect a wedding soon? – Yes, after my tour in August" (Z. 40–42)

zu 8: "I'm very lucky that he's prepared to travel with me, because it means that he had to give up his job." (Z. 54–56)

zu 9: "I was the lead singer of our school band. We gave concerts at our school, and did gigs in our area, such as weddings and large birthday parties." (Z. 66–69)

zu 10: "I know you're very rushed since you have a plane to catch." (Z. 75/76)

B Reading Comprehension

Hinweis: Im Prüfungsteil Leseverstehen begegnen dir bisweilen recht anspruchs-
volle Texte. Lass dich vom Umfang und sprachlichen Niveau dieser Texte nicht verunsichern, da du oftmals nicht jedes einzelne Wort verstehen musst, um die gestellten Aufgaben zu beantworten. Lies dir die Aufgaben aber immer gut durch, da hier
meist mehr Details als in den Hörverstehensaufgaben gefordert werden. Dafür hast
du aber auch die Möglichkeit, dir die Texte mehrmals genau durchzulesen.

1. Book reviews

Hinweis: Hier ist es hilfreich, in den Beschreibungen die Gewohnheiten und
Interessen der jeweiligen Person zu markieren. So hebst du wichtige Einzelheiten
hervor, die es dir erleichtern, das passende Buch zuzuordnen: "John (21) studies
law at university. In his free time he likes to read books about history, 16th century history in particular."

customer	❶	❷	❸	❹	❺
book	C	D	F	B	G

Hinweise:

zu 1: John interessiert sich für Geschichte, insbesondere für das 16. Jahrhundert.
Daher ist „Henry VIII and the Tudor Realm" das richtige Buch für ihn: "This
400-page volume deals with every aspect of sixteenth-century Tudor England [...]. A must-read for anyone interested in history."

zu 2: Julia hat einen anstrengenden Job und nicht viel Zeit zum Lesen. Daher
sind ihr Kurzgeschichten am liebsten. Sie sollte daher „David Patterson's" kau-
fen: " 'David Patterson's' consists of twenty-four short stories [...]. A perfect fit
for anyone short of time and in need of a rest in today's stressful world."

zu 3: Der Fremdenführer Ryan träumt davon, die Westküste der USA zu besu-
chen. „The Natural Beauties of San Francisco" wird ihn deshalb am meisten interessieren, da das Buch unter den aufgelisteten der einzige Reiseführer über
den amerikanischen Westen ist.

zu 4: Die Profi-Schwimmerin Kate liest gerne Bücher über exotische Tiere. Sie
sollte sich deshalb für „Finding Nemo – The True Story?" entscheiden: "Are
you interested in the sea? Would you like to find out more about the most exotic
fish around?" Der Band enthält darüber hinaus viele Fotos, was Kate begeistern
wird, da sie sich auch für Fotografie interessiert.

zu 5: Anthony hat auch nur wenig freie Zeit, die er zum Lesen nutzen kann. Da er Detektivgeschichten mag, wird ihm das Buch „The Secret Adventures of Sherlock Holmes" am besten gefallen: "Thirty-two short adventures, each consisting of about ten pages […]. The cases of this famous detective have been carefully reviewed and adapted to the twenty-first century."

2. School life abroad

Hinweis: Du hast jeweils vier Auswahlmöglichkeiten und musst die richtige Aussage ankreuzen. Lies den Text zuerst einmal ganz durch, damit du weißt, wovon er handelt. Beim erneuten Lesen markierst du am besten die entsprechenden Stellen im Text. Es kann sein, dass die falschen Antworten in einem anderen Zusammenhang im Text vorkommen; daher ist es äußerst wichtig, dass du den Text aufmerksam liest und auf Details achtest.

a) Tanja Huber
- ☐ was interviewed by a fifteen-year old girl.
- ☑ is from Germany.
- ☐ moved to England with her family.
- ☐ had a lot of problems at home.

Hinweis: "Tanja Huber […] is an ordinary fifteen-year-old girl from Fulda, Germany" (Z. 1/2)

b) Tanja's English
- ☑ is excellent.
- ☐ is not good.
- ☐ is average.
- ☐ could be better.

Hinweis: "When I met Tanja for the first time, I was impressed by her English." (Z. 5)

c) At the time of the interview, Tanja had already been in England for
- ☐ one month.
- ☐ four months.
- ☑ five months.
- ☐ seven months.

Hinweis: "During the first month in which I did a language course in London and my four months here in Bristol I've learned a lot" (Z. 5–7)

d) Tanja's brother is

- [ ] three years old.
- [ ] seven years old.
- [ ] fourteen years old.
- [✓] twenty-two years old.

Hinweis: "Tanja enjoys living with two 'sisters', as her own brother, who moved out three years ago, is <u>seven years older</u> than she is." (Z. 15/16) Da Tanja 15 Jahre alt ist (vgl. Z. 2) und einen sieben Jahre älteren Bruder hat, ist „twenty-two years old" die richtige Lösung.

e) The school uniform Tanja has to wear

- [ ] is green.
- [ ] is her least favourite colour.
- [✓] is white and blue.
- [ ] consists of a skirt and a blouse.

Hinweis: "I have to wear a blue skirt and blazer or pullover with the school's coat of arms and a white polo shirt." (Z. 21/22)

f) Registration

- [ ] is a type of training.
- [✓] is a way of finding out whether every pupil is in school.
- [ ] is a school uniform with the school's coat of arms.
- [ ] only takes place in the mornings.

Hinweis: "Every morning and every afternoon after lunch pupils have to go and register to show that they are in school. There is a quick registration in every lesson, too." (Z. 25–27)

g) Tanja goes to school

- [✓] by bike.
- [ ] without having had breakfast.
- [ ] after eating a full English breakfast.
- [ ] on her own.

Hinweis: "College is just a five-minute bike ride away" (Z. 31/32)

h) On school days, Tanja leaves the house

- [ ] at 8.15 a.m.
- [✓] at 8.45 a.m.
- [ ] at 9 p.m.
- [ ] at 8.45 p.m.

Hinweis: "before leaving the house with her 'sisters' at quarter to nine." (Z. 33/34)

i) The traditional English breakfast

- [ ] includes baked beans and fruit.
- [ ] includes bacon and cereal.
- [ ] is a healthy meal.
- [x] is also called "a fry-up".

Hinweis: "It was new to her that this hot breakfast is also called 'a fry-up'." (Z. 36/37)

k) After her GCSEs and some time abroad, Tanja will

- [ ] stay in Germany.
- [ ] train with a company in Australia.
- [ ] go back to Bristol.
- [x] go back to England.

Hinweis: "she wants to train with an English company after passing her GCSEs back in Germany and taking a gap year in Australia." (Z. 41/42)

3. An Unforgettable Trip to London

Hinweis: Lies den Tagebucheintrag zuerst einmal ganz durch, damit du weißt, was das Mädchen erlebt hat. Versuche dabei, die Hauptgedanken der Geschichte zu erfassen. Sollte ein dir unbekanntes Wort für das Verständnis des Textes wichtig sein, versuche zuerst, das Wort aus dem Sinnzusammenhang zu erschließen. Verstehst du es dann noch immer nicht, kannst du es in einem Wörterbuch nachschlagen.

a) The flat / Their flat is too small.
Hinweis: "As we live in a small flat, I couldn't have a big party" (Z. 3)

b) It was a trip to London.
Hinweis: "so my mum had saved up and had bought plane tickets for me and herself to London […] what a great surprise!" (Z. 3–6)

c) They went to the hotel bar to drink something. (Afterwards they went to bed.)
Hinweis: "As it was really late when we arrived at our hotel in the city centre, we had something to drink at the hotel bar and went straight to bed" (Z. 7–9)

d) the Houses of Parliament and the London Eye / Big Ben and the Tower
Hinweis: "We walked along the Thames up to the Houses of Parliament, heard Big Ben chime and went on the first ride of the London Eye" (Z. 10–12); "We got off at Tower Pier and visited the Tower …" (Z. 15)

e) They took the Tube and a boat. / They used the Underground and a ship.

Hinweis: „Tube" ist ein umgangssprachlicher Ausdruck für die U-Bahn in London: "we took the Tube to Knightsbridge." (Z. 17/18)
Obwohl im Text die Wörter „boat" oder „ship" nicht erwähnt werden, wird aus dem Textzusammenhang klar, dass Mutter und Tochter dieses Transportmittel auch benutzt haben: "I didn't want to go on a traditional sightseeing tour, so we went on a city cruise instead. Seeing London from the water was special." (Z. 13–15)

f) They went into Harrods.

Hinweis: "My mum insisted on going to Harrods" (Z. 18)

g) She thinks she saw Kate/Catherine, the Duchess of Cambridge.

Hinweis: "I suddenly saw an attractive brown-haired woman who looked just like Kate – I mean Catherine, the Duchess of Cambridge." (Z. 20–22)

h) They saw a crowd of people and the media waiting in front of a cinema.

Hinweis: "We were on our way back to the hotel, when we noticed a large crowd in front of one of the cinemas. We stopped to find out what was going on – lots of reporters, photographers and camera teams were standing at a red carpet." (Z. 24–27)

i) She wrote this, because her mother became very excited when she heard that some film stars were about to appear on the red carpet. Her mother started to check her appearance and made them wait for a long time, because she wanted to get an autograph, which is something a teenage girl would normally want. The girl, on the other hand, would have preferred to leave, because her feet were hurting.

Hinweis: "My mum suddenly got all excited; she checked her appearance and tried to get as close to the red carpet as possible. She is Richard Gere's biggest fan and was hoping to get an autograph. It was funny: I had the feeling that we had just switched roles. Suddenly I was the mother and she was an eighteen-year-old girl. Although our feet were killing us, my mum made us wait for the stars to appear" (Z. 29–34)

C Use of Language

1. Mediation

Hinweis: Eine Mediation ist keine reine Übersetzung. Vielmehr sollst du im ersten Teil (a–e) die gesuchten Informationen dem vorliegenden Material entnehmen und die Inhalte sinngemäß ins Deutsche übertragen. Im zweiten Teil (f–l) musst du in eigenen Worten auf Englisch formulieren.

a) 30 Minuten / eine halbe Stunde

    Hinweis: *"30 minutes flight time"*

b) Jugendliche unter 16 Jahren zahlen 15,50 £. Ab 16 kostet das Ticket 21,50 £. / Ab 16 Jahren muss man den vollen Preis (21,50 £) zahlen. / Ab 16 gilt man als Erwachsener und zahlt 21,50 £.

    Hinweis: Unter dem Punkt „Standard Ticket" steht, welche Personengruppen wie viel für ein Ticket bezahlen müssen: "Adults £ 21.50 [...] Children (4–15 years with valid ID) £ 15.50"

c) Man muss einen gültigen Personalausweis/Pass vorlegen.

    Hinweis: *"Children (4–15 years with <u>valid ID</u>) £ 15.50"*

d) am Kartenschalter, telefonisch und über die Website des London Eye

    Hinweis: *"To buy a ticket, go to our ticket office, call our booking line on +44(0)871 781 3000 or visit www.londoneye.com."*

e) mit der U-Bahn und mit dem Bus

    Hinweis: *"You can easily walk to the London Eye from several London <u>Underground</u> stations: [...] It is a short five-minute walk from Waterloo Station.";* *"<u>Bus</u> 211, 77 and 381. Most London sightseeing bus tours include the London Eye."*

f) Is it allowed/possible to take a (film) camera into the London Eye? /
Can you take a camera with you when you visit the London Eye? /
Are cameras allowed in the London Eye?

    Hinweis: „Mitnehmen" heißt im Englischen „to take (with you)". Die Übersetzung von „dürfen" ist von Kontext zu Kontext verschieden. Hier würde man „to be allowed to" oder „can" verwenden.

g) Is it true that many people get sick/nauseous when taking a ride with the London Eye? / Do many people get sick when they go on a ride with the London Eye?

    Hinweis: Hier wird nicht danach gefragt, wie vielen Leuten schlecht wird, sondern <u>ob</u> es viele sind.

h) Which celebrities have taken a ride with the London Eye? /
Can you tell me which famous people have been on the London Eye?

    Hinweis: Hier musst du das „present perfect" verwenden. Wenn du das englische Wort für „Prominente" („celebrities") nicht kennst, kannst du es mit „famous person/people" umschreiben.

i) Are there any movies/films where the London Eye can be seen? /
Can you tell me which films show/feature the London Eye? /
Do you know if there are films that show the London Eye?

k) It is a pity/It's too bad that your website is only in English. The information should be available/given in other languages too. / I suggest providing/translating the information on your website in other languages, too.

Hinweis: Der Ausdruck „etw. schade finden" wird üblicherweise mit „it is a pity" umschrieben. Lerne ihn am besten auswendig.

l) Thank you for taking the time to answer my questions. / Thank you for your time. / Thank you very much for answering my questions.

2. Words and structures

Hinweis: Im „Language"-Teil der Prüfung werden deine Kenntnisse in Grammatik und Wortschatz überprüft. Wenn du dir bei einer grammatikalischen Form nicht sicher bist oder die Lücke falsch ausgefüllt hast, schlage die entsprechenden Regeln in der Kurzgrammatik (auf der Onlineplattform MyStark) nach.

❶		❷		❸	
☐	to low	☐	with	☐	in general
✓	too low	☐	from	✓	generally
☐	much lower	✓	by	☐	general
☐	the lowest	☐	through	☐	by general
❹		❺		❻	
☐	on	☐	becomes	✓	experiment
✓	of	✓	became	☐	expertise
☐	from	☐	gets	☐	experiences
☐	to	☐	went	☐	exercise
❼		❽		❾	
☐	if	☐	mustn't	☐	had known
☐	as if	☐	will	✓	have been known
✓	when	✓	can	☐	had been known
☐	which	☐	needn't	☐	did know
❿		⓫			
☐	was	☐	as		
☐	where	☐	with		
✓	were	✓	which		
☐	have	☐	who		

Hinweise:

zu ❶: Du brauchst hier ein Adjektiv, das den Ton näher definiert. Die anschließende Phrase „to be detected" gibt den entscheidenden Hinweis, denn Infraschall ist zu schwach, um vom menschlichen Ohr wahrgenommen zu werden ("is too low to be detected"). Die Steigerungsformen „lower" und „the lowest" passen also hier nicht.

zu ❷: *Im Gegensatz zum Englischen sind im Deutschen mehrere Präpositionen möglich („mit dem menschlichen Gehör", „vom menschlichen Ohr", „durch das menschliche Gehör"). Bei „to be detected" handelt es sich aber um eine Passivkonstruktion, die den „by-agent" verlangt. Darum musst du hier „by" verwenden.*

zu ❸: *Bei dieser Lücke solltest du erkennen, dass sie sich innerhalb einer Verbphrase („it is … believed") befindet. Deshalb ist hier nur das Adverb „generally" möglich. Der Ausdruck „in general" könnte in diesem Satz nur verwendet werden, wenn sich die Lücke z. B. am Satzanfang befände. Das Adjektiv „general" würde nur in Verbindung mit einem Nomen funktionieren – ebenso die Konstruktion „by general" (z. B. „by general agreement").*

zu ❹: *Bei dieser Lücke geht es erneut um die richtige Präposition. Es liegt hier eine Genitivkonstruktion vor: Gavreau war einer der Pioniere der modernen Infraschallforschung. Der Genitiv muss in diesem Fall mit „of" gebildet werden.*

zu ❺: *Die Formulierung „anfangen, sich für etw. zu interessieren", die hier vervollständigt werden soll, benötigt entweder das Verb „to become" oder „to get". Die Zeitangabe „in the 1960s" ist jedoch ein Signal für „simple past", wodurch „became" die einzig mögliche Antwort sein kann.*

zu ❻: *Auf den ersten Blick sehen die vorgegebenen Wörter ähnlich aus, haben aber unterschiedliche Bedeutungen: „expertise" (= „wissenschaftliche Fachkenntnis"/„Kompetenz") und „exercise" (= „Übung") passen nicht in den Kontext und „experiences" (= „Erfahrungen") kann als Wort im Plural nicht auf den unbestimmten Artikel „an" folgen; nur „experiment" (= „Experiment") kann verwendet werden.*

zu ❼: *Es soll ein Nebensatz eingeleitet werden, der aber kein Relativsatz ist, weswegen man das Relativpronomen „which" ausschließen kann. Die beiden Möglichkeiten „if" („ob"/„falls") und „as if" („so, als ob") passen nicht in den Kontext. Bedenke ferner, dass „when" im Deutschen nicht nur mit „wann", sondern auch mit „als" übersetzt werden kann, wie in diesem Fall.*

zu ❽: *Hier fehlt der Verbkonstruktion ein Hilfsverb. Von den angegebenen passt nur „can", da Naturkatastrophen Infraschallwellen verursachen können.*

zu ❾: *Der Ausdruck „bekannt sein (für etw.)" wird im Englischen mit Passiv gebildet. Somit fallen die beiden Aktivformen „had known" und „did know" als mögliche Lösungen weg. Da die Aussage auch heute noch auf Elefanten zutrifft, ist nur die „present perfect"-Form „have been known" richtig: „Elefanten sind bekannt dafür, Infrasound aus zweieinhalb Meilen Entfernung hören zu können."*

zu ❿: *Aus dem Kontext erkennt man, dass es sich erneut um eine Passivkonstruktion handeln muss. Darüber hinaus wird der Plural („people at a concert") benötigt, weswegen „were" die richtige Lösung darstellt.*

zu ⓫*:* Im letzten Nebensatz handelt es sich um einen Relativsatz, der die Gefühle von Angst und Unsicherheit („feelings of uneasiness, fear and chills down the spine") genauer beschreibt. Somit musst du ein Relativpronomen verwenden. Da Gefühle keine Personen sind, kann man „who" als Pronomen ausschließen. Deswegen bleibt „which" als richtige Lösung übrig.

D Text Production

Hinweis: In der Textproduktion kannst du zwischen zwei Themen wählen. Lies zuerst beide Themen aufmerksam durch und überlege genau, welches dir mehr liegt. Achte beim Schreiben darauf, dass du die Vorgaben der Aufgabenstellung berücksichtigst. Lies am Ende noch einmal deinen ganzen Text konzentriert durch. Korrigiere dabei Grammatik- und Rechtschreibfehler. Überprüfe auch, ob der Text logisch aufgebaut ist.

Die Beispiellösungen sind etwas länger als die geforderten 150 Wörter, da hier auf alle Aspekte eingegangen wird. Du brauchst in deiner Antwort aber nur auf vier der fünf Fragen antworten.

How about Newcastle?

Hinweis: Du verfasst einen Brief an deinen Lehrer, in dem du dich um die Teilnahme am Schüleraustausch bewirbst. Denke daran, deine Adresse sowie die Angaben des Adressaten und das Datum zu ergänzen. Da es sich um einen formellen Brief handelt, solltest du keine Kurzformen verwenden.

(name of your school)   (your address)
(name of the English teacher)
(school address)

                                                                            (date)

Dear Mr (last name of the teacher),

My name is Max Richter and I am 16 years old. I am in class 10 A and I would love to take part in the exchange programme with the high school in Newcastle, because I have never been to England. Although languages are not my strength, I like my English classes and I am also interested in English history. I believe that I could improve my English if I were allowed to stay with an English host family for two weeks and go to school there.

In my free time, I like doing outdoor sports, like skateboarding or freerunning, but I also enjoy programming computer games. I have got a younger brother, Ben, who is always happy to test my games, and an older sister. Lena took part in the exchange programme three years ago. She has told me lots about it and she is still friends with her exchange partner. We have got a big house, so my exchange partner would even have his own room.

I would love to introduce him to my friends, show him around our town and go on some day trips, depending on what he would like to see.

Yours sincerely,
Max Richter *206 words*

An email to the Rocky Mountains Tourist Information Center

Hinweis: Du schreibst eine E-Mail an ein Informationszentrum für Touristen in den USA. Da du den genauen Adressaten nicht kennst, beginnst du einen Brief in der Regel mit „To whom it may concern" oder „Dear Sir or Madam" und beendest ihn mit „Yours faithfully".

To whom it may concern:

My name is Timo Wagner. I am a sixteen-year-old student from Germany. My friend Kai and I are planning a trip to the Rocky Mountains this summer. Both of us enjoy camping a lot and we think that the Rocky Mountains are an exciting destination, especially because neither of us has been to the United States before. However, we have got some questions to ask regarding our trip. As I already mentioned, we like camping, so it would be very kind if you could recommend some camp sites to us, especially those that are not too heavily frequented by tourists.

Furthermore, we would like to know whether there are guided tours for tourists, because my friend and I would like to see as much of the region as possible. We like hiking a lot, so we would love to go on a guided hiking tour far away from the usual tourist paths.

We would also appreciate any information concerning the issue of travel. Which is the nearest international airport? Which is the cheapest and quickest way to get to the Rocky Mountains from there?

Thank you very much for your help. I am looking forward to hearing from you soon.

Yours faithfully,
Timo Wagner *208 words*

A Listening Comprehension

Hinweis: Der Hörverstehenstest der Abschlussprüfung 2017 besteht aus drei Teilen. Alle Texte werden zweimal vorgespielt. Du kannst während des Abspielens jederzeit mit deinen Eintragungen beginnen. Im ersten Teil hörst du zwei Nachrichten. Der zweite Teil ist eine Umfrage und Teil 3 der „Listening Comprehension" ist ein Interview.

Part One

Hinweis: Du hast 20 Sekunden Zeit, um dir die Aussagen zu „News Item 1" durchzulesen. Während des ersten Hördurchgangs kannst du bereits mit Bleistift mögliche Antworten ankreuzen. Denke aber daran, deine endgültigen Antworten mit Füller oder Kugelschreiber festzuhalten. Jede richtige Antwort ergibt einen Punkt. Wenn du mehrere Antworten in einer Teilaufgabe ankreuzt, bekommst du keinen Punkt.

In „News Item 1" geht es um die längste Pizza der Welt, die 2016 unter der Mitarbeit von 250 Pizzabäckern in Neapel entstand. Deine Aufgabe ist es, zu erkennen, wie lang diese Pizza ist (a), wie viel Käse verwendet wurde (b), wann der Rekord der größten Pizza aufgestellt wurde (c) und womit die Pizza „Ottavia" belegt war (d).

Bevor du „News Item 2" hörst, hast du erneut 20 Sekunden Zeit, dir die vier Aussagen durchzulesen. Es geht hier um den ersten Roboter, der Pizzen ausliefert. Du musst erkennen, welchen Namen der Roboter hat (a), woraus seine Außenhülle besteht (b), was er kann (c) und was der Kunde tun muss, damit er seine bestellte Pizza erhält (d).

News Item 1

a) The world's longest pizza is _____ metres long.
- [ ] 250
- [✓] 1,850
- [ ] 2,000

Hinweis: "The delicious pizza was an impressive 1,850 metres long." (Z. 3/4)

b) The chefs used _____ kg of cheese.
- [ ] 200
- [ ] 1,600
- [✓] 1,950

Hinweis: "they used [...] 1,950 kg of cheese" (Z. 6/7)

c) The record for the world's largest pizza was set in
- [ ] 2000.
- [✓] 2012.
- [ ] 2016.

Hinweis: Hier musst du gut aufpassen, denn es geht nicht um die längste, sondern um die größte Pizza: "the title for the world's 'largest' has remained uncontested since 2012." (Z. 10–12)

d) The "Ottavia" was topped with
- [ ] meat.
- [ ] olive oil.
- [✓] lettuce.

Hinweis: "It was topped with […] 110 kilos of lettuce!" (Z. 15–18)

News Item 2

a) The new pizza delivery robot is called
- [ ] Carlo.
- [✓] CRU.
- [ ] Robotic Unit.

Hinweis: "Thanks to CARLO's Pizza Robotic Unit or CRU" (Z. 3/4)

b) The exterior of the robot is made of
- [✓] plastic.
- [ ] aluminium.
- [ ] steel.

Hinweis: "CRU's waterproof acrylic plastic exterior" (Z. 8)

c) The robot can
- [ ] order drinks.
- [ ] make hot pizzas.
- [✓] keep drinks cool.

Hinweis: "The robot […] has a separate cold area to accomodate drinks orders." (Z. 11–13)

d) In order to get the right pizza, the buyer must
- [✓] type in a number.
- [ ] order it from the robot.
- [ ] pick up the right one.

Hinweis: "To get their food, customers have to enter a code." (Z. 17)

E 2017-2

Part Two

Hinweis: Teil 2 ist eine Umfrage, in der sich sieben Personen zu Schuluniformen äußern. Die Aussagen der Befragten sind in Sprechblasen vorgegeben. Du musst die Aussagen den entsprechenden Personen zuordnen. Für jede richtige Zuordnung erhältst du einen Punkt. Beachte, dass eine Aussage zu viel ist und keinem der Sprecher zugeordnet werden kann.
Du hast zum Lesen der Aussagen 40 Sekunden Zeit. Unterstreiche Schlüsselwörter in den Sprechblasen, auf die du dich während des Zuhörens konzentrieren kannst.

Janet	Max	Kate	Robert	Amir	Mr Garland	Mr Slater
B	H	A	D	C	E	G

Hinweis
zu Janet: *"It makes me feel as if I belong somewhere" (Z. 14)*
zu Max: *"people get a better first impression of the school if the pupils all look the same." (Z. 18–20)*
zu Kate: *"It takes away my freedom to express myself as I want to." (Z. 27/28)*
zu Robert: *"it saves me time in the morning. I don't have to think about what I'm going to wear" (Z. 38/39)*
zu Amir: *"I sometimes have real problems when I come home from school. My uniform tells everyone that I go to a school for kids with lots of money." (Z. 51–54)*
zu Mr Garland: *"There are fewer conversations at the start of the day" (Z. 64/65)*
zu Mr Slater: *"We should be concentrating on smaller classes, better security in schools, more parental help and improved facilities." (Z. 74–76)*

Part Three

Hinweis: Im dritten Teil geht es um eine heldenhafte Katze, die ihre Familie aus ihrem brennenden Haus rettet, indem sie sie mitten in der Nacht weckt.
Du sollst in einer Tabelle jeweils nur eine Information angeben. Machst du mehrere Angaben und ist eine davon falsch, erhältst du keinen Punkt. Stichpunkte sind ausreichend, Zahlen musst du nicht ausschreiben. Pro Tabellenfeld wird maximal ein Punkt vergeben. Solange der Inhalt verständlich und korrekt ist, führen sprachliche Fehler nicht zu Punktabzug.

(1) why Claire woke up	**Tink/her cat jumped on(to) her legs/on her (bed)**
(2) how she realised something was wrong	**(there was a layer of white) smoke in her room/in the air/ the room was half-filled with (white) smoke**

E 2017-3

(3) what she did next	(she) woke (up) her partner/Russ/ (she) jumped out of bed/ (she) phoned the fire brigade
(4) where the fire had started	(at) (her/their) (next-door) neighbour's (house)/ neighbour
(5) Tink's condition after her rescue	(she) wasn't breathing/ (her) tongue was hanging out/ (she) stank of smoke/ (she) was (very) dirty but alive/ Claire thought she was dead
(6) Tink's hiding place in the kitchen during the fire	behind a cupboard (in the kitchen)/ behind a kitchen cupboard
(7) what the firefighter did for Tink	(he) carried her out of the house/ (he) put an oxygen mask on her/ (he) saved her life
(8) why Claire was particularly upset after the fire	(she had) lost all their/her/the photographs/photos
(9) how Tink behaved after the fire	(she was) timid/frightened/anxious/ (she) wouldn't get off Claire's knees/ (she) didn't want to get off Claire's knees/ (she) refused to get off Claire's knees/ (she) wanted to sit on Claire's knees/lap
(10) where they live now	(in) rented accommodation/ in a rented flat/house/ in a flat/house that/which they have rented

✐ Hinweis

zu 1: *"I was suddenly woken up by Tink, who had jumped up onto my legs." (Z. 9/10)*
zu 2: *Beachte, dass es hier um das Erkennen der Situation, nicht um das ungewöhnliche Verhalten der Katze geht: "but I soon realised something was very wrong. The room was half-filled with a layer of white smoke hanging in the air." (Z. 16–19)*
zu 3: *"I woke my partner, Russ, in a panic and we both jumped out of bed." (Z. 21/22) Beachte: Die Antwort "(she) phoned the fire brigade" wird zwar erst später im Text genannt (vgl. Z. 25), wird aber auch als richtig akzeptiert.*
zu 4: *"I realised that the source of the fire was actually our next-door neighbour's." (Z. 32–34)*

zu 5: *"Tink wasn't breathing and her tongue was hanging out." (Z. 45/46); "I thought she was dead!" (Z. 49/50); "She stank of smoke and was very dirty, but she was alive." (Z. 54/55)*

zu 6: *"She was lying behind a cupboard in the kitchen." (Z. 48/49)* Beachte: Nur das Wort „cupboard" reicht nicht aus, um einen Punkt zu erhalten.

zu 7: Die Aussage *"he went into the house again"* würde als Antwort nicht ausreichen, denn die Formulierung würde offenlassen, ob der Feuerwehrmann die Katze aus dem Haus retten bzw. wie er ihr helfen konnte: *"he came back out with Tink lying in his arms." (Z. 43/44); "The firefighter put an oxygen mask on her" (Z. 50/51)*

zu 8: *"I was especially upset because we had lost all our photographs." (Z. 62–64)*

zu 9: *"Tink had suffered too. She was timid and frightened. She refused to get off my knees when I tried to get up." (Z. 65–67)*

zu 10: Deine Lösung muss so formuliert sein, dass eindeutig hervorgeht, dass sie im Moment zur Miete wohnen: *"we have now moved into a rented accommodation" (Z. 69/70)*

B Reading Comprehension

1. What about a handshake?

Hinweis: Im ersten Teil des Leseverstehens sollst du die Überschriften (A–G) den Abschnitten (1–5) eines Textes zuordnen. Es gibt sieben Überschriften, aber nur fünf Textabschnitte. Für jede richtige Zuordnung bekommst du einen Punkt. Lies zunächst die Textabschnitte durch und suche nach Schlüsselwörtern, die du so oder in ähnlicher Weise in den Überschriften wiederfindest. Achte bei der Zuordnung darauf, dass die Überschrift alle Aspekte des Textabschnittes berücksichtigt.

part of the text	❶	❷	❸	❹	❺
heading	D	F	A	G	C

Hinweis

zu 1: Der Satz *"He has picked up the German habit of shaking hands with strangers, colleagues, friends – and family"* zeigt auf, dass das Leben in einem anderen Land ändern kann, auf welche Art und Weise man Menschen grüßt.

zu 2: Der Abschnitt beschreibt das Händeschütteln im Vereinigten Königreich: *"They do [shake hands], generally, when they meet someone for the first time. But they don't shake hands again at the end of the day […] nor do they shake hands with their parents [. . .]."* Somit ist Überschrift F richtig.

zu 3: Der gesamte Textabschnitt setzt sich mit der Thematik, wofür ein Hände-druck stehen kann, auseinander: "What do we really want to communicate in the first moments of meeting someone?" Dazu passt nur Überschrift A.

zu 4: Was man im Zusammenhang mit Händeschütteln tun und nicht tun sollte („Do's and don'ts"), wird in Abschnitt 4 z. B. mit "make sure your handshake is firm but not aggressive – three or four seconds is enough" beschrieben.

zu 5: Die Schlüsselstelle in Abschnitt 5 ist: "we need to know about local customs and how to use them". Im Text werden zahlreiche Beispiele aufgezeigt, wie man sich in unterschiedlichen Kulturkreisen begrüßt. Überschrift C hebt genau diesen Aspekt hervor.

2. Fun in mines

Hinweis: Hier wird im Multiple-Choice-Verfahren überprüft, ob du den Text verstanden hast. Es ist immer nur eine Antwort richtig, die den vorgegebenen Satzanfang ergänzt. Die Aufgaben sind in der Regel chronologisch angeordnet, d. h., die Antwort zur ersten Aufgabe findest du zu Beginn des Textes, die zur nächsten etwas weiter unten im Text usw. Lies dir zunächst den Text einmal kom-plett durch und lass dich nicht verunsichern, wenn du beim ersten Lesen nicht alles verstehst. Vieles lässt sich aus dem Kontext erschließen, wenn du dich intensiver mit den einzelnen Abschnitten beschäftigst. Beginne dann mit dem ersten Satz, den du ergänzen musst, und unterstreiche Schlüsselwörter. Lies danach den ersten Textabschnitt und markiere wichtige Stellen im Text. Auf diese Weise findest du die entsprechenden Textstellen schnell wieder, wenn du die Lösungen am Ende noch einmal überprüfst.

a) The Turda salt mine was closed for mining in
- [✓] 1932.
- [ ] 1939.
- [ ] 1945.
- [ ] 1992.

Hinweis: Die Antwort findest du direkt im ersten Abschnitt: "The mine [...] was shut in 1932" (Z. 2–4)

b) It was closed because

- [✓] mines nearby were more lucrative.
- [ ] it was needed as a bomb shelter.
- [ ] a cheese factory bought it.
- [ ] the city wanted to have a museum.

✏ **Hinweis:** Die Textstelle „*after competition from neighbouring mines rendered its operation unprofitable*" (Z. 4) verweist darauf, dass andere nahegelegene Bergwerke einträglicher waren.

c) Today, the Turda salt mine is

- [ ] used to excavate salt.
- [ ] a huge golf course.
- [✓] a popular theme park.
- [ ] a trampoline paradise.

✏ **Hinweis:** Der Text beschreibt in den Zeilen 8–11, dass das Bergwerk zu einem Museum und Vergnügungspark für Kinder umfunktioniert wurde.

d) The mine is also in _____ place of the world's most amazing locations.

- [ ] twentieth
- [✓] twenty-second
- [ ] sixtieth
- [ ] one hundred and twelfth

✏ **Hinweis:** "*is now ranked 22nd among the world's most spectacular destinations.*" (Z. 10/11)

e) In the park, you can

- [ ] play tennis, use paddle boats and jump on trampolines.
- [✓] swim, play tennis and go on a Ferris wheel.
- [ ] play minigolf, go on a Ferris wheel and take guided walking tours.

✏ **Hinweis:** Im Text findest du in den Zeilen 14–17 die Informationen, welche Aktivitäten der Park anbietet: „*includes a giant Ferris wheel, […] tennis courts*" (Z. 14/15); "*The mine even has […] a swimming pool*" (Z. 16/17).

f) In the Turda salt mine, people can admire tools of the past

- [✓] in the museum.
- [ ] in the Terezia mine.
- [ ] in the cone-shaped mine.
- [ ] on the magical lake.

✏ **Hinweis:** "*Adults and kids can learn about the history of the mine while admiring the perfectly preserved salt extracting equipment in the museum.*" (Z. 18/19)

g) The Llechwedd slate quarry features 3,000 square metres of
- ☐ slides.
- ☐ staircases.
- ☐ freshwater.
- ☑ bouncing nets.

Hinweis: *"the Llechwedd slate quarry has been converted into a trampoline paradise with over 3,000 square metres of netting." (Z. 22–24)*

h) Unlike the other mines, the Bonne Terre Mine offers
- ☐ a seventeen mile walk.
- ☐ scuba-diving in saltwater.
- ☑ scuba-diving in freshwater.
- ☐ walking tours underwater.

Hinweis: *"Visitors can take walking tours around what is believed to be the world's largest freshwater dive resort […] or even scuba dive in the crystal clear waters." (Z. 27–29)*

i) The special feature of the mine in Dahlonega is that
- ☑ people can look for gems.
- ☐ one can see how miners now live.
- ☐ it is a multi-coloured mining experience.
- ☐ you traverse a gold passage.

Hinweis: *"Here they will get an opportunity to learn how the ancient miners lived and also experience their day first-hand by panning for gold or mining for gems." (Z. 31–33)*

k) You could enjoy a choir concert in the
- ☐ Llechwedd slate quarry.
- ☑ Turda salt mine.
- ☐ Bonne Terre Mine.
- ☐ Consolidated Gold Mine.

Hinweis: *Hier musst du den ganzen Text überprüfen, um dieses Detail einer der Sehenswürdigkeiten zuordnen zu können. Die Antwort steht in Zeile 16, in der das Salzbergwerk von Turda näher beschrieben wird: "The mine even has a 180 seat amphitheatre for concerts and conferences".*

3. The Film Club

Hinweis: Lies den Romanauszug zunächst vollständig durch, damit du weißt, wovon der Text handelt. Anschließend liest du die Fragen, damit du beim zweiten Lesen des Textes die relevanten Stellen markieren kannst. Du musst nicht in vollständigen Sätzen antworten. Für sprachliche Fehler gibt es keine Punktabzüge, sofern man versteht, was gemeint ist, und sofern die Aussage dem Text sachlich entspricht.

a) She is (very) well-dressed / dressed to the nines. /
She is dressed really smartly. /
Her style is smart / chic. /
Her look is (quite) fashionable / stylish / elegant.
Hinweis: "Rebecca Ng [...] was dressed to the nines" (Z. 2). Du sollst hier <u>nicht</u> *die einzelnen Kleidungsstücke aufzählen, denn es geht um ihren Stil.*

b) It's dirty / messy / dark / a pit. /
The room is a mess / untidy. /
In his opinion, the bedroom is not fit to take a guest into. /
There are no windows. / There is no natural light.
Hinweis: "It was a pit down there. There were no windows, no natural light. Just a bed with a ratty green blanket, clothes on the floor, CDs splashed around the room" (Z. 6–8)

c) (they are)
– playing the bass (guitar)
– making music
– listening to music
– talking
– laughing
– singing
Hinweis: Hier musst du zwei Details nennen, die du in den Zeilen 13–15 findest. Aus dem Text geht nicht hervor, ob die beiden selbst Musik machen oder nur Musik hören. "You could hear Rebecca's voice floating above the music" (Z. 13/14) könnte sowohl bedeuten, dass sie singt, als auch, dass sie spricht. Deshalb werden alle diese Lösungsmöglichkeiten akzeptiert.

d) She has (got) a boyfriend (at the moment)./
   She had an older boyfriend before this one./
   She used to have a twenty-five-year-old boyfriend./
   The guys/boys are all over her like flies./
   She is very popular.

   Hinweis: Die Antwort auf diese Frage kannst du an folgenden Textstellen finden: "She's got a boyfriend, though." (Z. 17); "But the guy before him was twenty-five" (Z. 29); "She's got guys all over her, Dad. Like flies." (Z. 32)

e) He turns his head slightly to the side/sucks in his cheeks/purses his lips/frowns gravely.

   Hinweis: "Turning his head slightly to the side, he sucked in his cheeks, pursed his lips and frowned gravely. This was his 'mirror face'." (Z. 25–27) Hier genügt es, eine der oben genannten Antworten anzugeben, um den Punkt zu erhalten.

f) Jesse seems wiser/less (delusionally) vain than he was (at Jesse's age)./
   He seems to be wiser than his father/his dad./David./
   He appears less vain than David.

   Hinweis: "In that instant he seemed wiser than I was at his age. Less delusionally vain" (Z. 33)

g) He is nervous when he looks closely at her./
   He is/feels fine when he doesn't look closely at her. /
   Sometimes he is/gets nervous.

   Hinweis: "Not nervous or anything? […] – Just when I look closely at her. The rest of the time I'm fine." (Z. 38–40) Diese Textstelle beschreibt, wann Jesse nervös ist.

h) She is beautiful/(very) pretty/super attractive. /
   She looks sensational.

   Hinweis: Die Antwort auf diese Frage ist nicht wortwörtlich im Text zu finden. Du musst nach Aussagen im Text suchen, warum Jesses Vater den Begriff „knockout" in Bezug auf Rebecca verwendet. Gleich zu Beginn des Textes wird in den Zeilen 2 bis 4 Rebeccas Outfit beschrieben. In Zeile 23 sagt Jesse dann: "She's pretty, isn't she?" Du kannst also schlussfolgern, dass Rebecca „eine Wucht" ist, und ihr Aussehen auf Englisch mit aussagekräftigen Adjektiven beschreiben.

i) He is self-conscious / nervous. /
He is not quite sure what to think of the fact that a girl like Rebecca is / seems to be interested in him (and he desperately wants her to think he is cool). /
He wants to impress her.

Hinweis: Die Antwort auf diese Frage findest du nicht direkt im Text. Suche aber gezielt im letzten Abschnitt (Z. 36 – 42) nach relevanten Aussagen und gib in eigenen Worten wieder, warum Jesse seinen Vater über sein Verhalten gegenüber Rebecca befragt.

C Use of Language

1. Mediation – The school mediators

Hinweis: In der Mediation sollst du zwischen der Austauschschülerin Claire und den beiden deutschen Schülern Markus und Thomas dolmetschen. Achte immer genau auf die jeweils geforderte Zielsprache, die in den eckigen Klammern vor der Antwortzeile angegeben ist. Du sollst hier nicht alles Wort für Wort übersetzen, sondern wichtige Inhalte sinngemäß übertragen. Manchmal gibt es mehr als eine Möglichkeit, etwas in der Zielsprache auszudrücken.

Überlege genau, was die jeweilige Hauptaussage einer Äußerung ist. Diese musst du immer in die andere Sprache übertragen. Gehst du nicht auf den zentralen Aspekt einer Äußerung ein, bekommst du auf den gesamten Gesprächsbeitrag keinen Punkt.

Manchmal enthält eine Äußerung mehrere zusätzliche Aspekte. Entscheide dann, welche Aspekte für den Adressaten relevant sind. Ob z. B. die Jugendherberge, in der das Trainingswochenende für Streitschlichter stattfand, ein Schwimmbad hatte, ist völlig unwichtig und braucht nicht übertragen zu werden. Orientiere dich an den Punkten, die für den jeweiligen Gesprächsbeitrag vergeben werden. Diese geben dir Aufschluss darüber, wie umfangreich deine Lösung ausfallen sollte.

Gibst du Antworten in der falschen Zielsprache, bekommst du keinen Punkt. Achte bei der Übertragung der Inhalte auf die Perspektive des Sprechers. Verwendest du eine falsche Perspektive (egal, ob einmalig oder mehrfach), wird dir von der Gesamtpunktzahl der Mediation einmalig ein Punkt abgezogen.

Damit du dich schnell zurechtfindest, ist bei den Lösungen, die neben der Hauptaussage auch zusätzliche Aspekte enthalten, die Hauptaussage mit einem Sternchen (*) gekennzeichnet.

CLAIRE:	Hey you two. Why are you wearing those red pullovers?
DU [DEUTSCH]:	**Warum tragt ihr rote Pullover?/Claire möchte wissen, warum ihr zwei diese roten Pullover tragt. (1)**
MARKUS:	Hallo Claire. Wir sind die Streitschlichter an dieser Schule, und so können uns die anderen als Streitschlichter erkennen. Außerdem gefällt uns die Farbe.
DU [ENGLISCH]:	**They are the mediators/arbitrators at our school (1) and the other pupils/others can recognize them as mediators (when they are dressed) like this. (1)**

Hinweis: Dass den Streitschlichtern die Farbe gefällt, ist hier nicht wichtig.

CLAIRE:	Oh, I understand. And what exactly is your task? We don't have anything like that at our school. And by the way, German and American schools are so different!
DU [DEUTSCH]:	**Und was genau ist eure Aufgabe?/Was genau macht ihr denn da? (1*) So etwas gibt es an ihrer Schule nicht./An ihrer Schule gibt es nichts Vergleichbares./Deutsche und amerikanische Schulen sind so unterschiedlich./Sie findet, dass es große Unterschiede zwischen Schulen in Deutschland und Amerika gibt. (1)**
THOMAS:	Wir helfen Schülerinnen und Schülern, wenn sie Streit miteinander haben, eine Lösung für ihren Konflikt zu finden. Egal, ob Jungs oder Mädchen, Jüngere oder Ältere.
DU [ENGLISCH]:	**They help pupils who are having an argument to find a solution to their conflict./When pupils are arguing, they help them solve the conflict./They help pupils find a solution to their conflicts. (1)**

Hinweis: Dass die Streitschlichter für <u>alle</u> Schüler zuständig sind, braucht hier nicht erwähnt zu werden.

CLAIRE:	Really, and how did you learn that?
DU [DEUTSCH]:	**Und wie habt ihr das gelernt?/Woher wisst ihr, wie ihr das machen müsst/wie das geht? (1)**
MARKUS:	Wir haben an zwei Wochenenden ein spezielles Training mitgemacht. Dabei haben wir in Rollenspielen gelernt, wie man mit Schülerinnen und Schülern spricht. Am Ende gab es dann sogar einen kleinen Test. Das war ganz schön anstrengend, aber es hat sich gelohnt. Außerdem waren wir in einer tollen Jugendherberge, mit eigenem Schwimmbad. Das war wirklich super.

DU [ENGLISCH]: **They went on (two) special training weekends./They had two weekends of special training. (1*) They learnt/learned how to speak with pupils in role plays./In the end, there even was a short test./It was really exhausting, but worth it./They found it really hard, but it was worth it. (1)**

Hinweis: Die Hauptaussage ist, dass die Streitschlichter einen Wochenendkurs besucht haben. Diese Information musst du unbedingt ins Englische übertragen. Von den zusätzlichen Aspekten kannst du die Information übertragen, die dir sprachlich am leichtesten fällt bzw. die du für am wichtigsten hältst.

CLAIRE: Wow, that sounds really great. Can I come to your next meeting?

DU [DEUTSCH]: **Kann sie zu eurem nächsten Treffen kommen?/Sie fragt, ob sie zum nächsten Treffen kommen darf. (1)**

THOMAS: Ja, natürlich, wir treffen uns jeden ersten Donnerstag im Monat. Es gibt auch immer Kuchen und Limonade.

DU [ENGLISCH]: **Yes of course, they meet on the first Thursday every month. (1)**

CLAIRE: Well, that sounds really interesting. Thanks for the chat. Bye.

MARKUS: Bitte, tschüss!

2. Words and structures – Faces of India

Hinweis: In dieser Aufgabe werden deine Kenntnisse in Wortschatz und Grammatik überprüft. Lies den Text zuerst gut durch und trage die passenden Wörter aus der Box in die Lücken ein. Beachte, dass jedes Wort nur einmal verwendet werden darf und dass in der Box mehr Wörter stehen, als du benötigen wirst. Außerdem wird kein Punkt vergeben, wenn du das Wort falsch abschreibst. Achte darauf, dass einige Lücken am Satzanfang stehen und du das jeweilige Wort großschreiben musst.

India is an exciting country, with the Himalayas in the north and the paradise of Goa's beaches in the south. The tourist (1) **will** also find history and culture in the capital, New Delhi, and colourful nightlife and the Bollywood vibe in Mumbai, (2) **one** of India's most fascinating cities.

(3) **For** eighty-nine years, India was the "jewel in the crown" of the British Empire. That's why English – along with Hindi – is one of India's two major official languages. India has been an independent democracy (4) **since** 1947 – the biggest on the planet.

Today, with more than a billion people, India has one of the world's (5) **fastest** growing economies. Information technology, (6) **call**-centres and tourism are big business. Education is very important to produce the (7) **highly** qualified workers India needs.

Bollywood, the centre of India's film industry, makes around 900 films a year – and Indian music and dance, which are a big part of the films, (8) **continue** to be very popular. But that's not surprising because India has one of the youngest populations (9) **in** the world.

Rajasthan is a (10) **state** in north-western India. Here people still (11) **live** in mud-walled homes with no electricity or running water. Many children go to school, but others stay home to work, carrying water and firewood, (12) **tending** livestock and minding younger children.

Despite the (13) **hardships**, the villagers are extremely kind and generous and share chai (tea) or roti (bread) with every visitor.

Regardless where you go, India is a colourful and (14) **fascinating** place.

From: Spot On, 8/2009, pp. 10 –15

Hinweise:

zu 1: In diesem Satz wird dem Touristen eine Vorhersage gemacht, was er/sie dort vorfinden wird. Aus diesem Grund verwendet man hier das „will-future".

zu 2: Hier geht es um die Stadt Mumbai, die als eine von mehreren Städten beschrieben wird, die die größte Faszination auf Besucher ausüben. Der Superlativ „most fascinating" gibt dir den entsprechenden Hinweis auf das fehlende Wort.

zu 3: Die Präposition „for" hat viele Bedeutungen. Hier steht sie in Verbindung mit einer Jahreszahl und bezieht sich auf einen Zeitraum. Du hast wahrscheinlich gelernt, dass „for" ein Signalwort für das „present perfect" ist. Lass dich durch den Gebrauch der Zeiten in diesem Satz nicht verwirren: Das Wort „for" kann auch, wie hier der Fall, einen Zeitraum bezeichnen, der bereits abgeschlossen ist. Aus diesem Grund wird hier das Verb „(to) be" im „simple past" verwendet.

zu 4: Das Wort „since" ist ein Signalwort für das „present perfect", das in diesem Satz verwendet wird. Hier geht es um den Zeitpunkt, seit dem Indien eine Demokratie ist.

zu 5: Hier wird eine Steigerungsform benötigt. Das kannst du an der Konstruktion „one of the …" erkennen. Es fehlt somit der Superlativ eines Adjektivs. Die einzig passende Form ist „fastest".

zu 6: In diesem Satz geht es um erfolgreiche indische Wirtschaftszweige. Viele Firmen nutzen Dienstleister in Indien, die deren Kundenanrufe entgegennehmen. Wenn du nicht sofort auf „call-centres" kommst, kannst du nach dem Ausschlussprinzip vorgehen. Hilfreich ist darüber hinaus, dass auch im Deutschen das Nomen „Callcenter" gebräuchlich ist.

zu 7: Übersetzt du die der Lücke folgenden Wörter („qualified workers" = „qualifizierte Arbeiter/Arbeitskräfte"), erkennst du schnell, dass inhaltlich nur „highly" passt, denn „highly qualified" bedeutet „hoch qualifiziert". Grammatikalisch muss die Lücke mit einem Adverb gefüllt werden, denn das fehlende Wort beschreibt das Adjektiv „qualified" näher.

zu 8: Hier fehlt ein Verb im Plural, das sich auf „Indian music and dance" bezieht. Der Ausdruck „(to) continue to be popular" kann hier mit „weiterhin beliebt sein" übersetzt werden.

zu 9: Indien hat eine der weltweit jüngsten Bevölkerungen der Welt. Im Englischen verwendest du „*in* the world".

zu 10: Rajasthan ist ein Bundesstaat in Indien, was nur durch das Wort „state" ausgedrückt werden kann. Beachte, dass das Wort „land" in diesem Zusammenhang falsch wäre, da es sich hier nicht um Ackerland handelt.

zu 11: Das Wort „live" ist das richtige Verb, um auszudrücken, dass Menschen in Rajasthan in Lehmhütten leben.

zu 12: In diesem Satz findet man eine Aneinanderreihung von „present participles" („carrying", „minding"), die erläutern, welche Arbeiten viele Kinder in Rajasthan zu erledigen haben. Die „present participles" verkürzen hier einen Nebensatz. Daraus resultierend muss diese Lücke mit der Verbform „tending" ausgefüllt werden. Der Ausdruck „(to) tend livestock" bedeutet „das Vieh versorgen".

zu 13: Die Präposition „despite" bedeutet „trotz". Für die darauffolgende Lücke musst du nach einem Nomen suchen, das eine gegenteilige Bedeutung zum restlichen Inhalt des Satzes hat: Trotz vieler Entbehrungen („hardships") sind die Dorfbewohner sehr großzügig und teilen ihr weniges Essen mit den Besuchern.

zu 14: Das Nomen „place" gibt vor, dass in die vorangehende Lücke ein Adjektiv eingefügt werden muss. Von den hier möglichen Adjektiven passt nur „fascinating".

D Text Production

Hinweis: Du hast hier die Wahlmöglichkeit zwischen zwei Aufgaben. Die Textproduktion wird mit 25 Punkten, also einem Viertel der Gesamtpunktzahl, gewertet. Du kannst entscheiden, ob du eine Geschichte zu einem vorgegebenen Bild oder deine Gedanken zu einem Thema (hier: Die perfekte Abschlussfeier) schreiben möchtest. Du sollst ungefähr 150 Wörter schreiben und in deinem Text mindestens vier der fünf vorgegebenen Aspekte bzw. Fragen bearbeiten. Die Beispiellösungen hier sind etwas länger als die geforderten 150 Wörter, da hier auf alle Aspekte ausführlich eingegangen wird. Neben den Punkten für Inhalt (10 Punkte), Grammatik (5 Punkte) und Wortschatz (5 Punkte) gibt es weitere 5 Punkte für die Organisation deines Textes. Achte deshalb beim Schreiben darauf, dass dein Text klar strukturiert ist, d. h., es muss ein „roter Faden" durch Einleitung, Hauptteil und Schluss zu erkennen sein. Dein Text sollte darüber hinaus über Absätze eine äußerliche Struktur erhalten. Zähle abschließend die Wörter. Eine Überschreitung der geforderten Wortzahl ist zulässig, wenn dein Text durchgehend inhaltlich sinnvoll ist.

What is the story behind the picture?

✍ Hinweis: Verfasse eine E-Mail zu dem vorgegebenen Bild, auf dem sich sechs Personen mit Schwimmreifen an einem Strand befinden. Dazu solltest du das Bild erst einmal ganz genau betrachten und auf die kleinen Details (wie z. B. Ort, Gegenstände) achten. Lies dir die Aufgabenstellung und die gestellten Fragen gut durch und bearbeite mindestens vier der Fragen in deiner E-Mail.

TO: info@travel-online.com
SUBJECT: My unusual travel photo

Dear Sir or Madam,

I am writing to you to submit a photo from my last holidays, which I believe is quite unusual. The picture shows six people walking along a large beach in Spain. This in itself is not unusual. However, these people are carrying floating tyres and all of them are adults.

My little sister and I were lying on the beach, people watching, when suddenly this group walked right into our view. Seeing them coming along like this, one after the other, reminded me of a poster showing the Beatles walking on a zebra crossing, so I grabbed my camera and took the picture.

Of course, we continued watching them. When they went into the water, it became clear why they were equipped with floating tyres: they were all non-swimmers. Later, we talked to them and found out that they were a group of friends from Hong Kong who were travelling across Europe. Barcelona, which they had visited in the morning, was one of their many destinations. They only had a few hours before they had to board their bus to Madrid, but they did not want to miss the chance to jump into the Mediterranean Sea.

If you could publish my photo, I would be very pleased.

Yours faithfully,
Susi Schmitt

213 words

The perfect end-of-school party

✍ Hinweis: Bei dieser Aufgabenstellung sollst du eine perfekte Schulabschlussparty beschreiben. Bedenke unterschiedliche Möglichkeiten, wie du das Fest organisieren kannst, und begründe deine Auswahl. Lies dir deinen Text am Ende noch einmal aufmerksam durch und überprüfe, ob du ihn logisch aufgebaut hast.

After the final tests have been taken, it is time for the end-of-school party! Of course, it is important to start planning this important event a few months beforehand.

First, you have to agree on the ideal location. It is probably best to do some brainstorming and collect ideas. I would suggest an indoor location, because you do not want to be dependent on the weather. My year, for instance, has been lucky enough to rent a beautiful hall in our old post office. As the building is from the 1970s, it was a logical consequence that the motto would be "the 70s". I believe a fun motto is one of the reasons for a prom to be a huge success.

The choice of music is very important, too. Think carefully which kind of music everybody likes. For us, the decision was easy – we have a really cool teacher band playing cover songs from the 70s and a fantastic DJ leading us through the evening.

Food also plays an important role. Do you want a traditional dinner with people sitting at tables? Or do you want to offer finger food, which makes it easier for the guests to talk to many different people? Finger food is our preferred choice, by the way.

Another decision which you have to make is about the programme. It is important that the evening has a certain structure so nobody gets bored. We have put together a programme with our class teachers: First, the graduates are introduced, then we will receive our reports, followed by eating and dancing. As some parents still have a few outfits from the 70s, there will also be a best dressed competition at the end of the evening.

I really hope that our parties turn out to be perfect! *299 words*

A Listening Comprehension

Hinweis: Der Hörverstehenstest der Abschlussprüfung 2018 besteht aus drei Teilen. Alle Texte werden zweimal vorgespielt. Du kannst während des Abspielens jederzeit mit deinen Eintragungen beginnen. Im ersten Teil hörst du zwei Nachrichten. Der zweite Teil ist eine Umfrage und Teil 3 ist ein Interview.

Part One

Hinweis: Lies dir zunächst die Aufgaben zu „News Item 1" durch. Hierfür hast du 20 Sekunden Zeit. Während des ersten Hördurchgangs kannst du bereits mit Bleistift mögliche Antworten ankreuzen. Denke aber daran, deine endgültigen Antworten mit Füller oder Kugelschreiber festzuhalten. Jede richtige Antwort ergibt einen Punkt. Wenn du mehrere Antworten in einer Teilaufgabe ankreuzt, bekommst du keinen Punkt.

Im ersten „News Item" geht es um ein Gerät namens The Pilot. *Dies ist ein Kopfhörer, der Gespräche übersetzt. Deine Aufgabe ist es, zu erkennen, was* The Pilot *übersetzen kann (a), wie das Gerät aktuell funktioniert (b), welche Art von Gesprächen es übersetzt (c) und welche Sprachen kostenlos dabei sind, wenn du die* The Pilot *Kopfhörer kaufst (d).*

Bevor du „News Item 2" hörst, hast du erneut 20 Sekunden Zeit, dir die vier Sätze durchzulesen. Es geht hier um LiLou, das neueste tierische Mitglied der „Wag Brigade" des Flughafens in San Francisco. LiLou hilft Reisenden, sich wohler zu fühlen. Du musst erkennen, welcher Rasse LiLou angehört (a), was für ein Tier sie ist (b), welches spezielle Merkmal sie hat (c) und wo man sie außerhalb des Flughafens antreffen kann (d).

News Item 1

a) *The Pilot* can translate what you
- ☐ write.
- ☑ say.
- ☐ read.

Hinweis: "The Pilot [...] instantly translates <u>spoken</u> language." (Z. 8/9)

b) At the moment, the device works
  - ☑ only online.
  - ☐ only offline.
  - ☐ online and offline.

  Hinweis: *"the device is dependent on having a data connection, but developers hope that future generations of* The Pilot *will function offline too." (Z. 16–18)*

c) *The Pilot* translates
  - ☐ background conversation.
  - ☐ group conversations.
  - ☑ conversation between two people.

  Hinweis: *"*The Pilot *can only translate one-on-one conversations." (Z. 19/20)*

d) These languages are free with *The Pilot Translating Earpieces:*
  - ☑ French, Italian, Spanish and English
  - ☐ Arabic, Japanese, German and English
  - ☐ Russian, German, English and Arabic

  Hinweis: *"come with free access to French, Italian, Spanish, along with English." (Z. 25/26)*

News Item 2

a) LiLou is a
  - ☐ Labrador.
  - ☑ Juliana.
  - ☐ Chihuahua.

  Hinweis: *"LiLou is […] a Juliana." (Z. 5–7)*

b) She is a
  - ☐ dog.
  - ☐ traveller.
  - ☑ pig.

  Hinweis: *"LiLou is a small and colourful pig." (Z. 9)*

c) LiLou has
  - ☑ painted nails.
  - ☐ a toy guitar.
  - ☐ a bow on her tail.

  Hinweis: *"LiLou wears scarlet nail polish on her perfectly manicured nails." (Z. 16/17)*

d) When not at the airport, LiLou can often be found

☐ at training facilities.

☐ flying.

☑ in hospitals.

Hinweis: "When not helping calm nerves at the airport, LiLou can often be found entertaining the sick at local hospitals" (Z. 21–23)

Part Two

Hinweis: In Teil 2 hat ein Reporter sieben Personen zum Thema „Moderne Kommunikation" befragt. Die Aussagen der Befragten sind vorgegeben und du musst die Aussagen den entsprechenden Personen zuordnen. Für jede richtige Zuordnung erhältst du einen Punkt. Beachte, dass eine Aussage zu viel ist und keinem der Sprecher zugeordnet werden kann.

Du hast zum Lesen der Aussagen 40 Sekunden Zeit. Unterstreiche Schlüsselwörter in den Aussagen, auf die du dich während des Zuhörens konzentrieren kannst.

Jane	Graham	Mary	David	Rebecca	Mia	Sim
F	C	A	G	B	E	H

Hinweise:

zu Jane: "thanks to social media, I was able to keep in touch with friends [...] This made my situation easier." (Z. 12–15)

zu Graham: "I really do get fed up when I get messages which I can hardly understand because the spelling is so bad." (Z. 18–20)

zu Mary: "people find it increasingly difficult to communicate face to face." (Z. 26/27)/"They are unable to hold eye contact and they lack the social skills they need." (Z. 28/29)

zu David: "it does get on my nerves if I am out on a first date, for example, and the girl [...] spends more time on her phone than talking to me." (Z. 34–37)

zu Rebecca: "I think a mobile phone, which is designed to keep people connected, can actually drive us further apart." (Z. 38–41)

zu Mia: "You can quickly make a date, be spontaneous, change your mind or chat to several people at the same time." (Z. 47–49)

zu Sim: "when I start my homework, I have to put my phone in another room. It's so tempting to pick it up." (Z. 50–52)

Part Three

Hinweis: Der dritte Teil ist ein Interview. Ein Reporter spricht mit einer Mutter, die sich dazu entschied, ihren Kindern eine außerordentliche Lektion zu erteilen, indem sie sechs Tage lang im Haushalt streikte.

Lies die Anweisungen genau durch und ergänze die gewünschten Informationen in der Tabelle. Du sollst jeweils nur eine Information pro Zeile angeben. Machst du mehrere Angaben und ist eine davon falsch, gibt es keinen Punkt. Stichpunkte sind ausreichend, Zahlen musst du nicht ausschreiben. Pro Tabellenfeld wird maximal ein Punkt vergeben. Sprachliche Fehler führen nicht zum Punktabzug, solange der Inhalt verständlich und korrekt ist.

(1) what Jessica means by 'going on strike'	(She) stop(ped) cleaning up / tidying up.
(2) why this was necessary	The house was always a mess. / Her children did not tidy up (after themselves).
(3) what was wrong in the house (2 aspects)	• (The) breakfast / dinner dishes were on the table. • (The) dishwasher was full / overflowing. • Dirty socks (were) on the floor. • (Used) tissues (were) on the sofa. • (The) children's shoes / backpacks were in the hall.
(4) what the dog did	(It) lick(ed) the dirty plates clean.
(5) what happened on Day Four	(The youngest) daughter / One of her daughters / Quinn cried / broke down / picked her stuff up around the house / asked her mom for help.
(6) why Jessica ended the strike	(Her / The) children were beginning to blame each other / fight.
(7) what she did while the children were tidying up	(She) sat on the couch / (she) drank coffee.
(8) what the children now do to help	(They) (now) rinse the breakfast dishes / put the breakfast dishes in the dishwasher / empty their lunchboxes.
(9) why Jessica can feel proud of herself	(Her) children are now more independent / will be able to look after themselves.

✏ **Hinweise:**
zu 1: *"I decided to go on strike and stop tidying up and cleaning up after the children." (Z. 17/18)*
zu 2: *"The house was in a real mess and none of it was from me." (Z. 14/15)*
<u>Beachte</u>: *Die Antworten „the kids should take responsibility" und „to teach the kids*

a lesson" sind ebenfalls richtig. Diese Formulierungen sind zwar nicht wörtlich im Text enthalten, inhaltlich aber korrekt.

zu 3: *"the breakfast dishes and the dinner dishes were still on the table, all crusty. The dishwasher was overflowing and the children's shoes and backpacks were in the middle of the hall." (Z. 26–30)/ "there were dirty socks on the floor and used tissues on the sofa." (Z. 39/40)*

<u>Beachte</u>: für die alleinige Antwort „dirty socks" gibt es keinen Punkt.

<u>Beachte</u> zu Fragen 2 und 3: Für die Antwort „in a real mess" kann nur ein Punkt vergeben werden.

zu 4: *"the dog had licked clean the dirty plates in the dishwasher." (Z. 42/43)*

<u>Beachte</u>: Die Antwort „the dog cleaned the plates" ist sinngemäß falsch, hierfür gibt es keinen Punkt.

zu 5: *"Quinn broke down crying and said [...] 'Can you please help me to clean up?' And she went around picking up her things." (Z. 53–57)*

<u>Beachte</u>: Die Antwort „the (youngest) daughter/Quinn didn't want to eat off paper plates" ist auch richtig und ergibt einen Punkt.

zu 6: *"I stopped the strike because the children were beginning to fight and blame each other." (Z. 64–66)*

zu 7: *"I just sat on the couch and drank coffee which my daughters had made for me" (Z. 72/73)*

<u>Beachte</u>: Auch für die Antwort „not a thing"/„nothing" gibt es einen Punkt.

zu 8: *"They do now rinse their breakfast dishes and put them in the dishwasher and they empty their lunchboxes from the day before." (Z. 79–82)*

zu 9: *"You have made them more independent" (Z. 83/84)/ "one day, they will be able to look after themselves." (Z. 85/86)*

B Reading Comprehension

1. Tennis star Andy Murray and the science of success

   Hinweis: Im ersten Teil des Leseverstehens geht es darum, Überschriften (A–G) den Abschnitten eines Textes (1–5) zuzuordnen. Es gibt sieben Überschriften, aber nur fünf Textabschnitte. Für jede richtige Zuordnung bekommst du einen Punkt. Lies zunächst die Textabschnitte durch und suche nach Schlüsselwörtern, die du so oder in ähnlicher Weise in den Überschriften wiederfindest. Achte bei der Zuordnung darauf, dass die Überschrift alle Aspekte des Textabschnittes berücksichtigt.

part of the text	❶	❷	❸	❹	❺
heading	G	D	E	A	B

Hinweise:

zu 1: Dieser Textabschnitt verweist auf den „osmolarity check", einen Test, mit dem der Urin von Andy Murray untersucht wird.

zu 2: Der gesamte Textabschnitt beschreibt, welche Ernährungsvorschriften von Murray eingehalten werden und was er zu welcher Tageszeit zu sich nimmt.

zu 3: Hier wird erklärt, dass er eine zitronengelbe Mischung aus speziellen Inhaltsstoffen trinkt.

zu 4: In Textabschnitt 4 geht es um Murrays „Background-Team", das aus sechs Personen besteht: "Six people spend their lives assessing and checking his body."

zu 5: Dieser Textabschnitt beschreibt, dass sich Murrays mentale Vorbereitung geändert hat, seit ihn Ivan Lendl trainiert: "the difference [Ivan Lendl] has made to Murray's mental preparation has been significant"

2. Toxic e-waste dumped in poor nations

Hinweis: Hier wird im Multiple-Choice-Verfahren überprüft, ob du den Text verstanden hast. Es ist immer nur eine Antwort richtig, die den vorgegebenen Satzanfang ergänzt. Die Aufgaben sind in der Regel chronologisch angeordnet, d. h. die Antwort zur ersten Aufgabe findest du zu Beginn des Textes, die zur nächsten etwas weiter unten im Text usw. Lies dir zunächst den Text einmal komplett durch. Lass dich nicht verunsichern, wenn du beim ersten Lesen nicht alles verstehst. Wenn du dich intensiver mit den einzelnen Abschnitten beschäftigst, lässt sich vieles aus dem Kontext erschließen. Beginne mit dem ersten Satz, den du ergänzen musst, und unterstreiche darin Schlüsselwörter. Lies dann den ersten Textabschnitt und markiere wichtige Stellen im Text. Auf diese Weise findest du die entsprechenden Textstellen schnell wieder, wenn du deine Lösungen am Ende noch einmal überprüfst.

a) The UN reports that electronic rubbish
   - ☑ is taken to less developed countries.
   - ☐ is dumped in developed countries.
   - ☐ was bought this Christmas.
   - ☐ has caused a flood.

   Hinweis: "electronic waste (e-waste) [...] is being <u>dumped illegally in developing countries</u>" (Z. 2/3)

b) The amount of e-waste will

- [ ] weigh as much as an Egyptian pyramid.
- [ ] be stored near the Egyptian pyramids.
- [✓] increase in the near future.
- [ ] be tackled by the UN programme.

✏ **Hinweis:** *"The global volume of electronic waste is expected to grow by 33 percent in the next four years"* (Z. 4/5). Dieser Satz beschreibt, um wie viel Prozent der Elektronikmüll in den nächsten vier Jahren, d. h. in naher Zukunft, zunehmen wird.

c) Last year, _____ of e-waste were made.

- [ ] more than 50 million tonnes
- [ ] about seven million kilograms
- [✓] about 50 million tonnes
- [ ] less than seven million kilograms

✏ **Hinweis:** *"Last year, nearly 50 million tonnes of e-waste were generated worldwide"* (Z. 6)

d) One problem is that

- [ ] workers in Europe suffer from illness.
- [✓] poisonous substances escape into the environment.
- [ ] electronic goods contain toxic substances like copper.
- [ ] mobile phones in use pollute land, water and air.

✏ **Hinweis:** *"these toxic materials seep out into the environment"* (Z. 11)

e) Nowadays,

- [✓] electronic goods do not last long.
- [ ] technical innovation is slowing down.
- [ ] TVs and mobile phones pollute the environment.
- [ ] TVs and mobile phones explode.

✏ **Hinweis:** *"TVs, mobile phones and computers are all being replaced more and more quickly. The lifetime of products is also shortening."* (Z. 15/16)

f) In 2015, _____ produced the most electronic rubbish.

- [ ] the United States
- [ ] Europe
- [✓] China
- [ ] Germany

✏ **Hinweis:** *"China produced 11.1 million tonnes in 2015, followed by the US with 10 million tonnes"* (Z. 18/19)

g) Another problem is that
    [✓] a lot of e-waste is not recycled properly.
    [ ] only 33 % of e-waste is recycled.
    [ ] millions of phones were collected and recycled.
    [ ] millions of phones were collected in Latin America.

    Hinweis: Im Text findest du die Information, dass jährlich hundert Millionen Handys weggeworfen oder in Schubladen gelegt werden, statt sie an Sammelstellen abzugeben und entsorgen zu lassen: "many hundreds of millions [of mobile phones] are thrown away each year or are left in drawers." (Z. 29/30)

    Außerdem wird ausgeführt, dass in den USA nur wenig recycelt wird: "the US threw away 258.2 million computers, monitors, TVs and mobile phones in 2015, of which only 66 percent were recycled." (Z. 25–27)

h) In 2016,
    [ ] 12 million new mobile phones were sold.
    [ ] 12 million new mobile phones were bought in the US.
    [ ] 120 million mobile phones were recycled in the US.
    [✓] 120 million mobile phones were sold in the US.

    Hinweis: "In the US, only 12 million mobile phones were collected for recycling in 2016, even though 120 million were bought." (Z. 30/31)

i) Phones and other electronic devices
    [ ] are becoming less complicated.
    [✓] contain precious metals such as gold.
    [ ] have circuit boards made of lithium.
    [ ] have silver coatings.

    Hinweis: "Most phones contain precious metals. The circuit board can contain copper, gold, zinc and others." (Z. 34/35)

k) If we do not change our habits,
    [ ] some materials needed for electronic devices will boom.
    [ ] there will be a shortage of electronic inventions.
    [✓] there will be a shortage of rare-earth elements.
    [ ] there will be no rare-earth elements left.

    Hinweis: "The failure to recycle is also leading to shortages of rare-earth elements" (Z. 39)

3. The lifeboat clique

Hinweis: Lies den Romanauszug zunächst vollständig durch, damit du weißt, wovon der Text handelt. Anschließend liest du die Fragen, damit du beim zweiten Lesen des Textes die relevanten Stellen markieren kannst. Du musst nicht in

*vollständigen Sätzen antworten. Für sprachliche Fehler gibt es keine Punktabzü-
ge, sofern man versteht, was gemeint ist, und sofern die Aussage dem Text sachlich entspricht.*

*Beachte: Schau genau, aus welcher Perspektive die Fragen gestellt sind und be-
antworte sie entsprechend. Beispielsweise wird Frage a) aus der Perspektive
Denvers gestellt („What does Denver think?") und du musst folglich mit „she"
antworten, auch wenn im Text natürlich „I" steht. Ist die Perspektive in deinen
Antworten durchgehend falsch gewählt, wird dir ein Punkt von der Gesamtpunktzahl abgezogen. Wechselst du die Perspektive jedoch mehrfach, wird dir
bei jeder einzelnen Aufgabe ein Punkt abgezogen.*

a) She hated it from the start./LA can turn on you if you're not on your guard.
   *Hinweis: "and I hated it from the start." (Z. 2)/"LA can turn on you if
   you're not on your guard." (Z. 5)*

b) (The worst is) if they don't think anything/if they think nothing.
   *Hinweis: "worst of all – if they don't think anything about you."
   (Z. 10/11)*

c) The tables are set out in a grid./Students are designated by tables.
   *Hinweis: "Our high school lunchroom was set out in an orderly grid. [...]
   the students were carefully designated by tables" (Z. 20–22)*

d) – geeks
   – losers
   – student council
   – (deeply committed) Christians
   – drama students
   – young felons
   – the most popular kids
   *Hinweis: Hier musst du zwei der genannten Personengruppen angeben.
   Du findest sie alle in den Zeilen 22–28.*

e) (She sits) at one of the uncategorized tables/with other students who don't
   really fit into a group/with students who eat their lunch fast.
   *Hinweis: "and several uncategorized tables, where I sat with various oth-
   er students who didn't really fit into a group and who ate their lunch fast"
   (Z. 24–26).*

f) – They are in the eleventh grade/the most popular kids/a group of sixteen
   – They have got the shiniest teeth/the best hair/the fastest cars/the sleekest
     abs.
   *Hinweis: Hier musst du nur zwei charakteristische Eigenschaften nennen,
   die du in den Zeilen 27–30 findest.*

g) She cannot be herself./Nobody is really interested in her./She has to play a designated role./She is ruled by others./She feels helpless./She wants school to be as painless as possible.

Hinweis: In den Zeilen 6–14 beschreibt Denver, was für sie „sleepwalking" bedeutet. Denke nach, was sie damit meinen könnte, und beschreibe dann einen der Aspekte.

h) She feels jealous of Abigail./She dislikes/hates Abigail./She admires Abigail secretly because Abigail is the "star" at the table./She thinks Abigail is stupid or silly./She can't understand why a girl like Abigail is so popular.

Hinweis: Die Antwort auf diese Frage ist ebenfalls nicht direkt im Text enthalten. Suche im letzten Abschnitt (Z. 29–34) nach Aussagen, in denen Denver Abigail beschreibt. Davon ausgehend musst du dir überlegen, was diese Beschreibung bedeuten könnte. Wenn Denver z. B. von „stupid parties" (Z. 33) spricht, kann das bedeuten, dass sie diese Partys tatsächlich blöd findet, aber auch, dass sie neidisch ist und eigentlich auch gerne eingeladen wäre. Wie bei g) musst du also auch hier den Text selbst interpretieren.

C Use of Language

1. Mediation – Traditional festivities

Hinweis: In der Mediation sollst du zwischen dem schottischen Austauschschüler Jake und einem Passanten dolmetschen. Achte immer genau auf die geforderte Zielsprache (Deutsch oder Englisch?), die in den eckigen Klammern vor der Antwortzeile angegeben ist. Es muss dabei nicht alles Wort für Wort übersetzt werden. Manchmal gibt es mehr als eine Möglichkeit, etwas auszudrücken. Beachte, dass hier zwischen Hauptaussagen und weiteren Aspekten unterschieden wird. Die Hauptaussage musst du immer in die andere Sprache übertragen. Nennst du keine der Hauptaussagen, so wird der jeweilige Gesprächsbeitrag mit null Punkten bewertet, selbst wenn die Nebenaspekte sachlich richtig sind.
Damit du dich schnell zurechtfindest, ist bei den Lösungen, die neben der Hauptaussage auch zusätzliche Aspekte enthalten, die Hauptaussage mit einem Sternchen (*) gekennzeichnet. Außerdem ist in Klammern angegeben, für welche Aussagen du Punkte erhältst.
Gibst du Antworten in der falschen Zielsprache, bekommst du ebenfalls keinen Punkt. Achte auch auf die Perspektive des Sprechers. Verwendest du eine falsche Perspektive (egal ob einmalig oder mehrfach), wird dir von der Gesamtpunktzahl der Mediation einmalig ein Punkt abgezogen.

Jake:	I keep seeing this poster for a "Hutzelfeuer". What is that?
Du [Deutsch]:	**Was ist ein „Hutzelfeuer" (1)?**
Passant:	Ach, das Plakat. Das sieht sehr schön aus, nicht wahr? Beim „Hutzelfeuer" werden die alten Weihnachtsbäume verbrannt. Das Feuer soll den Winter vertreiben. „Hutzelfeuer" ist echt ein komisches Wort. Ich weiß nicht, wo es herkommt.
Du [Englisch]:	**Old Christmas trees are burned (on a fire). / They / We burn old Christmas trees. (1) The fire is meant to drive out the winter. / We celebrate it to end the season. (1)**
Jake:	Oh, I see. That sounds fun. What a nice way to end a season! What other customs do you have here?
Du [Deutsch]:	**Welche anderen Bräuche gibt es hier (bei uns) / haben wir hier (bei uns)? (1)**
	Hinweis: Die Begriffe „Traditionen" und „Feste" anstelle von „Bräuche" für „customs" sind auch richtig.
Passant:	Lass mich mal überlegen. Das größte Ereignis hier bei uns ist die „Kirmes". Da bauen wir ein Zelt auf und abends spielen Bands. Das ganze Dorf kommt zusammen und wir freuen uns schon das ganze Jahr darauf! Letztes Jahr war ich mit meiner gesamten Familie dort, obwohl es ganz schön kalt war.
Du [Englisch]:	**The biggest event (here) is "Kirmes". / The biggest thing (here) is "Kirmes". (1*) We / They put up a tent / and there are bands in the evening(s). The whole village comes together and everybody looks forward to it all year. (1)**
Jake:	That sounds like great fun.
Passant:	Falls er dann noch hier sein sollte, muss er unbedingt hingehen. Das wird ihm gefallen. Gibt es etwas Ähnliches da, wo er herkommt?
Du [Englisch]:	**Is there anything like that where you are from? (1)**
Jake:	I don't think so, but "Burns Night" is very important where I come from. This is a celebration in honour of the Scottish poet Robert Burns. He's probably the most well-known poet of Scotland. "Burns Night" is celebrated at the end of January every year.
Du [Deutsch]:	**Nein, es gibt nichts dergleichen, aber „Burns Night" ist sehr wichtig, (1*) wo er herkommt. Es ist eine Feier zu Ehren des schottischen Dichters Robert Burns. Burns Night wird immer Ende Januar gefeiert. (1)**
Passant:	Das finde ich sehr ungewöhnlich. Was passiert denn an „Burns Night"? Komisch, dass ich noch nie davon gehört habe, wenn das in Schottland so eine große Sache ist.

Du [Englisch]:	**What happens on "Burns Night"? (1)**
Jake:	We always eat "haggis", mashed potato and turnips. Then there are speeches and whisky and people recite poems by Burns. I was sorry to miss it this year. My brother told me all about it.
Du [Deutsch]:	**Sie essen immer „Haggis", Kartoffelbrei und Rüben. (1) Und außerdem werden Reden gehalten und es gibt Whisky. (1) Die Leute tragen Gedichte von Burns vor/sagen Gedichte von Burns auf. (1)**
	Hinweis: Schreibst du nur „Sie essen immer Haggis" ohne den Zusatz „Kartoffelbrei und Rüben", gibt es keinen Punkt.
Passant:	Das hört sich richtig interessant an. Danke für das Gespräch!

2. Words and structures – Coral reefs in danger

Hinweis: Diese Aufgabe überprüft deine Kenntnisse in Wortschatz und Grammatik in Form eines Lückentextes. Lies den Text zuerst einmal komplett, bevor du mit der Bearbeitung der Aufgaben beginnst. Für jede Lücke sind vier Antwortmöglichkeiten vorgegeben. Lies die möglichen Lösungen genau durch. Wenn du dich für eine Antwort entschieden hast, überprüfe deine Wahl noch einmal anhand des Ausschlussverfahrens. Für jede richtige Antwort bekommst du einen Punkt.

1.		2.		3.		4.	
	for	✓	people		is		takes
✓	of		peoples		was	✓	paints
	from		people's	✓	has been		brushes
	off		peoples'		had been		pictures
5.		**6.**		**7.**		**8.**	
✓	which		upset		later		adding
	who	✓	urgent		further	✓	including
	what		unless	✓	sooner		incorporating
	where		urban		afterwards		excluding
9.		**10.**		**11.**		**12.**	
	protected	✓	effects		situations		won't act
	protection		conclusions		positions		didn't act
	protecting		meanings		country	✓	don't act
✓	protect		impressions	✓	places		hadn't acted

Hinweise:

zu 1: Nur of *ist richtig, denn die übrigen Präpositionen ergeben mit dem Verb* to be in danger *keinen Sinn, da* to be in danger of *eine feststehende Wendung ist, die immer mit der -ing-Form steht.*

zu 2: Das Nomen people *ist ein Pluralwort und wird mit „Leute", „Menschen" übersetzt. Das Wort* peoples *ist hier falsch, da es mit „Völker" übersetzt wird. Die Wörter* people's *und* peoples' *haben jeweils ein Genitiv-s und ergeben hier keinen Sinn.*

zu 3: Hier passt nur has been, *also das „present perfect", da am Satzanfang das Signalwort* For *(„seit") steht.*

zu 4: Hier passt nur das Verb paints, *da* to paint a grim picture *(„ein düsteres Bild zeichnen") eine feste Wendung ist.*

zu 5: Zu many of *passen nur* which *und* who. *Das Relativpronomen* who *wird ausschließlich bei Personen verwendet,* which *aber bei Sachen. Somit ist* which *richtig, da sich das gesuchte Relativpronomen auf das Nomen* places *bezieht.*

zu 6: Das Wort urgent *(dringend) ist das einzige, das in diesem Zusammenhang einen Sinn ergibt.* upset *bedeutet „verärgert",* unless *„außer" und* urban *„städtisch".*

zu 7: Nur sooner *ist richtig, da die anderen Lösungsmöglichkeiten inhaltlich nicht passen.*

zu 8: Wenn du den Kontext genau beachtest, wirst du feststellen, dass nur die Präposition including *infrage kommt. Die Ozeane sind der Lebensraum für 1 Million Arten, zu denen auch ein Viertel aller Fische weltweit gehört.*

zu 9: Mit diesem Satz wird eine Tatsache ausgedrückt, die dauerhaft gültig ist. Deswegen musst du das „simple present" einsetzen.

zu 10: Inhaltlich passt in diese Lücke nur effects, *weil es um die <u>Auswirkungen</u> des Schwundes von Riffen geht.*

zu 11: Das Wort places *ist das richtige Nomen, um auszudrücken, dass Menschen von einigen Orten wegziehen müssen, denn hier sind keine Situationen, Positionen oder Länder gemeint.*

zu 12: Hier liegt ein If-Satz Typ I vor, den du am „will future" im Hauptsatz erkennst. Beim Typ I musst du das „simple present" im Nebensatz einsetzen.

D Text Production

✎ *Hinweis: Im letzten Teil der Prüfung, der Textproduktion, hast du eine Wahlmöglichkeit zwischen zwei Aufgaben. Dieser Teil wird mit 25 Punkten, also einem Viertel der Gesamtpunktzahl, gewertet. Du kannst entscheiden, ob du eine Geschichte zu einem vorgegebenen Bild oder einen Artikel für deine Schülerzeitung (hier: Thema „Schlafgewohnheiten") schreiben möchtest. Du sollst ungefähr 150 Wörter schreiben und in deinem Text auf mindestens vier der fünf vorgegebenen Aspekte bzw. Fragen eingehen. Neben den Punkten für Inhalt (10 Punkte), Grammatik (5 Punkte) und Wortschatz (5 Punkte) gibt es weitere 5 Punkte für den Aufbau deines Textes. Achte deshalb beim Schreiben darauf, dass dein Text klar strukturiert ist, d. h., es muss ein „roter Faden" durch Einleitung, Hauptteil und Schluss zu erkennen sein. Dein Text sollte darüber hinaus über Absätze eine äußerliche Struktur erhalten. Zähle abschließend die Wörter. Du darfst die Wortzahl überschreiten, wenn dein Text durchgehend sinnvoll ist und es zu keinen Wiederholungen kommt.*

What is the story behind the picture?

✎ *Hinweis: Da es hier um kreatives Schreiben geht, kannst du deiner Fantasie freien Lauf lassen und deine Lösung kann auch dann gut sein, wenn sie inhaltlich von dem hier abgedruckten Lösungsvorschlag abweicht. Achte aber in jedem Fall darauf, vier der vorgegebenen Aspekte abzudecken und das Bild genau anzuschauen, damit dein Text plausbibel ist.*

These two people you can spot in the picture are my friend Julie and me. The photo was taken by another friend, Cathy. Last summer holidays the three of us visited Julie's Aunt Mary in Boston and this is where this snapshot was taken.

We were on our way back home from the shopping mall and we were late for dinner. That is why we thought we should take a shortcut. However, this wasn't one of our best ideas … We lost our way and ended up in a blind alley with that high fence. However, behind the fence the way moved on and the map showed us that it was just one block away from Aunt Mary's. So we decided to climb the fence when suddenly the police stopped us and asked what we were doing there. We explained our problem and because we were tourists, they gave us a ride back home. Aunt Mary wasn't so happy about it, but for Julie, Cathy and me, it was an unforgettable memory of these holidays. *175 words*

A good night's sleep

✎ *Hinweis: Beachte, dass du von deiner eigenen Erfahrung, dass einige Schüler*innen zu wenig schlafen, ausgehen kannst. Du kannst und sollst also auch persönliche (ggf. erfundene) Informationen, z. B. zu deinem Schlafverhalten und zu deiner Meinung, warum viele Teenager spät schlafen gehen, anbringen.*

A good night's sleep

One of my classmates fell asleep during Maths last week. This led me to write this article about students' sleeping habits.

Didn't my classmate get enough sleep at night? I cannot imagine sleeping at school, because I do not have any sleeping problems at all. Normally I go to bed early. So I have some more time to read a book, if I like, or I fall asleep immediately. Therefore, I get more than enough sleep and I am well-rested in the morning. We teenagers need to sleep, it is no waste of time. The advantages of sleeping well are obvious: you are not that tired in the morning, you are more concentrated at school and you still have time during the day to enjoy your hobbies. However, some students go to bed late in the evening because they forget the time while playing computer games or watching TV.

Dear fellow students, to avoid embarassing situations like falling asleep during lessons, be responsible and do not go to bed too late. *171 words*

A Listening Comprehension

Hinweis: *Der Hörverstehenstest der Abschlussprüfung 2019 besteht aus drei Teilen. Alle Texte werden zweimal vorgespielt. Du kannst während des Abspielens jederzeit mit deinen Eintragungen beginnen. Im ersten Teil hörst Du zwei Nachrichten. Der zweite Teil ist eine Umfrage und Teil 3 der „Listening Comprehension" ist ein Interview.*

Part One

Hinweis: *Lies dir zuerst die Aussagen zu „News Item 1" durch. Dafür hast du 20 Sekunden Zeit. Während des ersten Hörens kannst du bereits mit Bleistift mögliche Antworten ankreuzen. Denke aber daran, dass du deine endgültigen Antworten mit Füller oder Kugelschreiber festhältst. Jede richtige Antwort ergibt einen Punkt. Wenn du mehrere Antworten in einer Teilaufgabe ankreuzt, bekommst du keinen Punkt.*
Im ersten „News Item" geht es um die „10,000 Year Clock", eine Uhr, die 10 000 Jahre lang in Betrieb sein soll. Deine Aufgabe ist es, zu erkennen, in welchen Abständen sich der Uhrzeiger bewegt (a), wann die Arbeiten an der Uhr begonnen haben (b), woher die Uhr ihre Energie bekommt (c) und was die Hoffnungen des Geldgebers Jeff Bezos sind (d).
Bevor du „News Item 2" hörst, hast du nochmals 20 Sekunden Zeit, dir die vier verschiedenen Aussagen durchzulesen. Es geht hier um den „π-Tag". Du musst erkennen, wer oder was an diesem Tag genau gefeiert wird (a), zu welcher Tageszeit der Wettbewerb startet (b), was man an diesem Tag in Princeton machen kann (c) und von wem die Zahl π zuerst genau berechnet wurde (d).

News Item 1

a) The clock hand moves once every
   ☐ year.
   ☑ one hundred years.
   ☐ one thousand years.

Hinweis: *"It also has a clock hand that moves once every one hundred years"*
(Z. 3/4)

b) Work on the clock started in

☐ 1995.

☐ 2000.

☑ 2011.

Hinweis: "*it was not until 2011 […] that work on a full-scale version of the 10,000 Year Clock began properly.*" *(Z. 8–11)*

c) The clock gets its power from

☑ changes in temperature.

☐ giant gears and dials.

☐ solar energy.

Hinweis: "*Its power comes from thermal energy captured by changes in day and nighttime temperatures on the mountain top.*" *(Z. 17–19)*

d) Jeff Bezos hopes the clock will

☐ connect with future generations of clocks.

☑ change how we think about time.

☐ never be repeated.

Hinweis: "*Bezos says he hopes the clock will 'change the way humanity thinks about time'*" *(Z. 22–24)*

News Item 2

a) Pi Day celebrates

☐ the scientist Albert Einstein.

☐ delicious American pies.

☑ a famous number.

Hinweis: "*Everybody knows that pi is the number 3.14*" *(Z. 1)*

b) In Los Angeles, the pie-eating competition begins

☐ in the afternoon.

☐ in the evening.

☑ at night.

Hinweis: "*a pie-eating contest, which begins at 1:59 am*" *(Z. 9/10)*

c) On Pi Day in Princeton, you can

☐ practice your math.

☑ dress up as Albert Einstein.

☐ make pies.

Hinweis: "*take part in an Einstein lookalike contest.*" *(Z. 20/21)*

d) Pi was first calculated accurately by the

- ☑ Greeks.
- ☐ Egyptians.
- ☐ Babylonians.

Hinweis: *"It was the Greeks, however, who first worked out pi accurately"* *(Z. 26/27)*

Part Two

Hinweis: *Teil 2 ist eine Umfrage, bei der sich sieben Personen zum Thema „Sommerferien" äußern. Die Aussagen der Befragten sind in Sprechblasen vorgegeben. Du musst die Aussagen den richtigen Personen zuordnen. Für jede richtige Zuordnung erhältst du einen Punkt. Beachte, dass eine Aussage zu viel ist und nicht zugeordnet werden kann.*

Du hast zum Lesen der Aussagen 40 Sekunden Zeit. Unterstreiche Schlüsselwörter in den Blasen, auf die du dich während des Zuhörens konzentrieren kannst.

Rosie	David	Jessica	Dean	Kendra	Mark	Emily
D	B	H	A	E	C	G

Hinweise:

zu Rosie: *"I enjoyed learning Spanish and I made lots of new friends."* *(Z. 11/12)*

zu David: *"But my parents …! In the evenings, I had to be back in my room by 10 pm. I was so angry about that"* *(Z. 18–20)*

zu Jessica: *"I went to the island of Corfu with some friends […] There are discos and great bars full of young people."* *(Z. 23–27)*

zu Dean: *"I prefer holidays with my friends too. If you don't feel like surfing, however, there is […] kayaking and stand-up paddling or simply just chilling out at a beach café."* *(Z. 30–36)*

zu Kendra: *"my mum kept borrowing my clothes and my dad acted as if he was 19."* *(Z. 39–41)*

zu Mark: *"I love family holidays. We often go hiking and cycling in Snowdon National Park in Wales."* *(Z. 45–47)*

zu Emily: *"Working abroad also gives you the feeling of being on holiday"* *(Z. 56–58)*

Part Three

Hinweis: Der dritte Teil ist ein Interview mit einer Parkour-Athletin, die von ihrer Karriere als Freerunnerin erzählt.
Lies die Anweisungen genau durch und ergänze die gewünschten Informationen. Du sollst in der vorgegebenen Tabelle jeweils nur eine Information angeben. Machst du mehrere Angaben und ist eine davon falsch, gibt es keinen Punkt, auch wenn die richtige Angabe dabei ist. Stichpunkte reichen aus, Zahlen musst du nicht ausschreiben. Pro Tabellenfeld wird maximal ein Punkt vergeben. Sprachliche Fehler führen nicht zu Punktabzug, solange der Inhalt verständlich und korrekt ist.

(1) where she found out about freerunning	**(at) university/gym sessions**
(2) what sport she did before freerunning	**cheerleading/gym sessions/gymnastics**
(3) types of work (2 details)	• **advertising (campaigns)** • **films** • **TV (shows)** • **live performances** • **stunts (for actresses)** • **doubling actresses**
(4) most exciting thing about her job	**travel(ling)**
(5) training (2 details)	• **a lot (of training)/hard (training)** • **in the gym** • **on the streets** • **an hour or two most evenings** • **pull-ups** • **(10 kg) weights** • **running**
(6) number of Internet followers	**(over) 160,000**
(7) how you can get involved in freerunning	**(look for) classes online/(find out if there is a) parkour community (near you)/online tutorials**
(8) what she loves about the sport	**(There are) no limitations/no rules./You can train anywhere./(You can be) creative.**

Hinweise:

zu 1: "It all started while I was at university." (Z. 15)/"I went along to gym sessions and that's where I met a group of guys who did freerunning." (Z. 18–20)

zu 2: "I started cheerleading … I went along to gym sessions" (Z. 17/18)

zu 3: "You have taken part in **advertising campaigns** and in **films**. You have also been on **TV** and **performed live**." (Z. 33–35)/"I have done **stunts** for various actresses […] I **doubled** Milla Jovovich" (Z. 37–39)

zu 4: "The most exciting thing about my job […] is that it allows me to travel so much." (Z. 41–43)

zu 5: "A lot! I work hard in the gym as well as on the streets […] I do an hour or two most evenings, doing pull-ups and 10 kg weights, as well as running" (Z. 48–52)

zu 6: "you have 160,000 followers online" (Z. 56/57)

zu 7: "I would look for classes online." (Z. 60)/"find out whether there is a parkour community near where you live." (Z. 62–63)/"There are loads of tutorials online" (Z. 66)

zu 8: "there are no limitations, no rules. You can train anywhere […] It's all down to your own creativity." (Z. 70–73)

B Reading Comprehension

1. Somalia's team on ice

Hinweis: Im ersten Teil des Leseverstehens musst du die Überschriften (A–G) den Textabschnitten (1–5) zuordnen. Es gibt sieben Überschriften, aber nur fünf Textabschnitte. Für jede richtige Zuordnung bekommst du einen Punkt. Lies zunächst die Textabschnitte durch und suche nach Schlüsselwörtern, die du so oder in ähnlicher Weise in den Überschriften wiederfindest. Achte bei der Zuordnung darauf, dass die Überschrift alle Aspekte des Textabschnittes berücksichtigt.

part of the text	❶	❷	❸	❹	❺
heading	E	D	A	G	B

Hinweise:

zu 1: Dieser Textabschnitt verweist auf die wachsenden Anfeindungen, denen Geflüchtete ausgesetzt sind. Manche nach Schweden geflohene Somalier*innen haben zum Beispiel Morddrohungen erhalten oder wurden Opfer von Brandstiftungen.

zu 2: Der gesamte Textabschnitt beschreibt, wie Hans Grandin nach Ideen zur Integration in seinem Heimatort suchte und diese im Sport fand. Es gab zuvor schon ein Fußballteam Geflüchteter und nun wollte Grandin ein Team aus Geflüchteten zusammenstellen, das die Sportart Bandy betreibt.

zu 3: Abschnitt 3 erklärt das Spiel Bandy, das Fußball recht ähnlich ist, und beschreibt, dass die größte Schwierigkeit darin liegt, sich schnell auf dem Eis zu bewegen und mit dem Schläger zurechtzukommen.

zu 4: Im Textabschnitt 4 geht es darum, dass das somalische Bandy-Team Mitglied in der Internationalen Bandy-Föderation wurde und 2014 an der Weltmeisterschaft teilnahm. Obwohl das Team sehr schlecht war (*"We hold the record for the world's worst team ever to play in the championship"*), wurde es zur Mediensensation.

zu 5: Mursal Ismail beschreibt in diesem Texabschnitt, dass es, obwohl sein Team hart trainiert, nicht nur um den Sport geht, sondern auch darum, etwas für Schweden zu tun, Feindseligkeiten abzubauen und somalische Geflüchtete in die Gesellschaft zu integrieren.

2. **The story of circus**

   Hinweis: Hier wird im Multiple-Choice-Verfahren überprüft, ob du den Text verstanden hast. Es ist immer nur eine Antwort richtig, die den vorgegebenen Satzanfang ergänzt. Die Aufgaben sind in der Regel chronologisch angeordnet, d. h. die Antwort zur ersten Aufgabe findest du zu Beginn des Textes, die zur nächsten etwas weiter unten im Text usw. Lies dir zunächst den Text einmal komplett durch. Wenn du beim ersten Lesen nicht alles verstehst, lass dich nicht verunsichern. Wenn du dich intensiver mit den einzelnen Abschnitten beschäftigst, lässt sich vieles aus dem Kontext erschließen. Beginne mit dem ersten Satz, den du ergänzen musst, und unterstreiche Schlüsselwörter. Lies dann den ersten Textabschnitt und markiere wichtige Stellen im Text. Auf diese Weise findest du die entsprechenden Textstellen schnell wieder, wenn du die Lösungen am Ende noch einmal überprüfst.

   a) Philip Astley's performances included
   - ☐ trapeze acts, acrobats and riding stunts.
   - ☑ horse-riding, acrobats and clowns.
   - ☐ tightrope walking, clowns and tumbling.
   - ☐ horse-riding, human cannon balls and trampolines.

   Hinweis: "performing trick riding stunts" (Z. 4) und "acrobats and clowning were part of the mix." (Z. 5/6)

b) The name "circus" was first used in
- [ ] 1768.
- [✓] 1782.
- [ ] 1793.
- [ ] 1825.

Hinweis: *"The first structure to be called a circus, however, was the Royal Circus, built in 1782" (Z. 7)*

c) The first circus tent was built by
- [ ] Charles Hughes.
- [ ] John Bill Rickets.
- [✓] Joshua Purdy Brown.
- [ ] Philip Astley.

Hinweis: *"Joshua Purdy Brown erected the first circus tent" (Z. 12)*

d) The use of tents enabled circuses to
- [ ] develop trapeze acts.
- [ ] associate with European circuses.
- [ ] perform in a sawdust ring.
- [✓] perform in all weathers.

Hinweis: *"The tent was one of the most important features in allowing circus to […] do shows regardless of rain or storm." (Z. 14–16)*

e) Jules Léotard trained using
- [ ] thick mattresses.
- [ ] no protection at all.
- [ ] the safety net.
- [✓] his father's pool.

Hinweis: *Jules Léotard nutzte zum Training den Pool seines Vaters, um bei Abstürzen den Aufprall mithilfe des Wassers abzufangen: "by hanging swings above his father's swimming pool […] The water broke his frequent falls during training." (Z. 18/19)*

f) Zazel, the first human cannonball, performed her act until
- [ ] she was shot in Mexico.
- [ ] she missed the safety net.
- [ ] the cannon failed.
- [✓] she had an accident.

Hinweis: *"She continued to perform her act […] until her career was ended when she was shot from a cannon in New Mexico, the net failed and she got hurt." (Z. 24–26)*

g) Clowns have been part of the circus since
- [✓] its beginning.
- [ ] 1830.
- [ ] 1900.
- [ ] 1984.

Hinweis: "Right from its start, clowns began entertaining audiences" (Z. 28/29)

h) Circuses gained in popularity after the introduction of
- [ ] the safety net.
- [✓] train tracks.
- [ ] elephants.
- [ ] the big top.

Hinweis: In den Zeilen 31–34 wird aufgezeigt, dass mit dem Bau der Eisenbahn Zirkusse an Popularität gewannen, da sie nun sehr weit reisen konnten: "Without the <u>railways</u>*, circus would never have become such a popular entertainment in the US." (Z. 33/34)*

i) Since 1984, elements of modern circus have often included
- [ ] wild animals.
- [ ] a sawdust ring.
- [✓] theatre.
- [ ] clowns.

Hinweis: "Its modern, dazzling, high-quality acts with theatrical elements" (Z. 35/36)

k) Many people stopped going to the circus because
- [ ] the ticket prices went up.
- [ ] of a new wild animal act.
- [✓] they couldn't see elephants anymore.
- [ ] the Ringling Brothers gave their last performance.

Hinweis: Seitdem der „Ringling Brothers Circus" in seiner Show keine Elefanten mehr zeigt, verkauft er weniger Eintrittskarten: "there had been a sharp drop in ticket sales after the company stopped using elephants." (Z. 39/40)

3. Winter classroom

Hinweis: Lies den Romanauszug zunächst vollständig durch, damit du weißt, wovon der Text handelt. Lies anschließend die Fragen, damit du beim zweiten Lesen des Textes die relevanten Stellen markieren kannst. Du musst nicht in vollständigen Sätzen antworten. Für sprachliche Fehler gibt es keine Punktabzüge, sofern man versteht, was gemeint ist, und sofern die Aussage dem Text sachlich entspricht.

a) – the gifted/talented kids
    – the hockey players
    Hinweis: *"The gifted and talented kids" (Z. 2/3)/"The hockey players" (Z. 5)*

b) – They sleep (in class)/take naps (during lessons).
    – They eat chips (in class).
    – They don't pay attention/dream of Empire.
    – They don't fill in worksheets/hand in blank worksheets.
    Hinweis: *"The hockey players had to be prodded awake" (Z. 5)/"They woke from her naps" (Z. 7)/"to dump open bags of chips into their mouths" (Z. 8)/"and return to their dreams of Empire." (Z. 9)/"They got teachers to forgive their blank worksheets" (Z. 11)*

c) She thinks that it would make the students listen better/pay attention to the lesson/try harder to understand./She has a tic.
    Hinweis: *"Ms. Lundgren had a tic. Whenever she got irritated or inspired, she switched instantly to whispering. She thought that would make us listen better; she thought it would make us pay attention [...]; she thought we would try harder to understand" (Z. 19–22)*
    Beachte: Für eine Antwort in der falschen Perspektive, z. B. *"make us listen"*, wird kein Punkt vergeben.

d) It no longer holds any relevance for her./It's boring/unimportant for her.
    Hinweis: *"and it was like hearing some obscure rumor that [...] no longer held any relevance we could make out." (Z. 23–25).*

e) – There is a lot of snow/four feet of snow./The snow blows away in gusts./The snow drifts are as high as houses.
    – There are strong winds/storms.
    – It's very cold./There is strong frost/windchill.
    – It's beautiful when the sun shines.
    Hinweis: Hier musst du zwei Details für den Winter in Minnesota angeben *"Outside: four feet of snow sealed in a shiny crust." (Z. 15)/"you could see snow blow away in gusts, then drift back the next day in piles as high as houses." (Z. 26/27)/"a late-season storm" (Z. 28)/"windchill" (Z. 36)/"the sun came out: brilliant, stunning us all." (Z. 35)*

f) The school needs them to win the District Championship./The school doesn't want to lose the District Championship again./They are very important to the school.
    Hinweis: *"The hockey players had to be prodded awake when the stack came down their aisle, had to be treated with great deference – or else we would lose the District Championship. Again." (Z. 5–7).* Diese Textstelle zeigt, wie wichtig es für die Schulgemeinschaft ist, die Meisterschaft zu gewinnen.

Daraus kannst du schließen, dass die Lehrkräfte den Mitgliedern des Hockey-
teams schlechte Schulleistungen nachsehen, damit sie sich auf ihre sportlichen
Leistungen konzentrieren können.

g) The lesson is boring and any distraction more than welcome./She hasn't seen
the blue car/the person before and is wondering what she or he is doing
there./It's a small town and strangers arouse curiosity.

Hinweis: Die Antwort auf diese Frage steht nicht direkt im Text. Lies dir
besonders die letzten beiden Abschnitte nochmals durch und überlege, was der
Grund dafür sein könnte, dass Madeline den Vorgang draußen so gespannt
beobachtet. Mögliche Antworten sind, dass sie den Biologieunterricht lang-
weilig findet und sich ablenken möchte oder dass sie neugierig auf die ihr un-
bekannte Person draußen ist.

C Use of Language

1. Mediation – Volunteer work

Hinweis: In der Mediation sollst du zwischen Tiffany und Claudia dolmetschen.
Achte immer genau auf die jeweils geforderte Zielsprache, die in eckigen Klam-
mern angegeben ist. Du musst dabei nicht alles Wort für Wort übersetzen. Manch-
mal gibt es mehr als eine Möglichkeit, etwas auszudrücken.
Beachte, dass hier zwischen Hauptaussagen und weiteren Auspekten unterschie-
den wird. Die Hauptaussage musst du immer in die andere Sprache übertragen.
Nennst du die Hauptaussage nicht, so wird der jeweilige Gesprächsbeitrag mit
null Punkten bewertet, selbst wenn die Nebenaspekte richtig sind.
Damit du dich gut zurechtfindest, ist bei den Lösungen, die Haupt- und Nebenas-
pekte enthalten, die Hauptaussage mit einem Sternchen (*) gekennzeichnet. Au-
ßerdem ist in Klammern angegeben, für welche Aussagen du Punkte erhältst.
Gibst du Antworten in der falschen Sprache, bekommst du ebenfalls keinen Punkt.
Achte bei deinen Übersetzungen auf die Perspektive der Erzählerin. Verwendest
du eine falsche Perspektive (egal ob einmalig oder mehrfach), wird dir von der
Gesamtpunktzahl der Mediation einmalig ein Punkt abgezogen.

Tiffany: I understand that Claudia is doing some volunteer work here on
the island. Could you ask her what kind of volunteer work that is?

Du [Deutsch]: Welche Art freiwillige Arbeit machst du gerade hier? (1)

Hinweis: Die Antwort „Ehrenamt" anstelle von „freiwilliger
Arbeit" ergibt ebenfalls einen Punkt.

Claudia:	Ich mache ein sogenanntes Freiwilliges Ökologisches Jahr. Nach der Schule wusste ich nicht genau, was ich weiter machen sollte – da habe ich schon erst mal in der Luft gehangen. Aber da ich mich schon immer für Naturschutz interessiert hatte, dachte ich, das Freiwillige Ökologische Jahr wäre die perfekte Sache für mich.
Du [Englisch]:	**She is doing a voluntary ecological year. (1*).** **She didn't know what to do when she finished school. <u>or</u>: As she had always been interested in the protection of nature, this appeared to be perfect to her. (1)**
Tiffany:	Oh, that sounds interesting. Especially in such a beautiful place! What are her tasks here on the island?
Du [Deutsch]:	**Was sind (denn) deine Aufgaben (hier auf der Insel)? (1)**
Claudia:	Hauptsächlich mache ich Führungen. Besonders mag ich die Besuche von Schulklassen, denn die Kinder sind immer so begeistert! Manchmal muss ich auch noch Büro- und Gartenarbeiten machen. Das macht mir nicht immer so viel Spaß, muss aber auch sein … man kann ja nicht alles haben.
Du [Englisch]:	**She mainly gives guided tours. (1) Sometimes she has to do office work and gardening too. (1)**
	✎ Hinweis: Welche Aufgaben Claudia Spaß machen und welche weniger, ist hier nicht wichtig.
Tiffany:	Wow, that's truly impressive. What has been the most exciting thing that has happened to her so far?
Du [Deutsch]:	**Und was war die aufregendste Sache, die dir bisher passiert ist? (1)**
Claudia:	Das war vor zwei Wochen, als Touristen ein verlassenes Seehundbaby am Strand meldeten. Ich schnappte mir sofort das Fernglas und rannte los, um das zu überprüfen. Zum Glück war es ein falscher Alarm und die Mutter holte das Kleine ab.
Du [Englisch]:	**Tourists found an abandoned baby seal on the beach. (1*) Fortunately, it was a false alarm and the mother came and got the baby seal. (1)**
	✎ Hinweis: "fake alarm" statt "false alarm" ist auch richtig.
Tiffany:	Wow, that sounds really exciting. We saw some of them today. They are so cute.
Claudia:	Tiffany wirkt so überrascht. Gibt es so etwas Ähnliches nicht auch in Amerika?
Du [Englisch]:	**Isn't there something like this in America/the USA? (1)**

Tiffany:		Not exactly. But we do have the "Peace Corps", where you can volunteer for projects around the world. Last year, a friend of mine went to Tanzania, a country in Africa, to build water tanks. What she told me about that experience really impressed me.		
Du [Deutsch]:		**Nicht genau so, aber es gibt das „Peace Corps", bei dem man als Freiwillige oder Freiwilliger in Projekten auf der ganzen Welt arbeiten kann. (1*) Letztes Jahr war eine Freundin von ihr in Tansania/Afrika und hat dort Wassertanks gebaut./ Eine Freundin von ihr hat sie mit ihrem Einsatz in Afrika beeindruckt. (1)**		
Claudia:		Das hört sich aber auch spannend an! Ich bin froh, dass ich euch getroffen habe. Lasst uns doch unsere Nummern austauschen und in Kontakt bleiben.		
Du [Englisch]:		**She wants to stay in touch and exchange/swap (phone) numbers. (1)**		
Tiffany:		Great idea! Here is my number! I'll give her my e-mail address too!		

2. Words and structures – Getting kids interested in chemistry

✐ *Hinweis: Diese Aufgabe überprüft deine Kenntnisse in Wortschatz und Grammatik in Form eines Lückentextes. Für jede Lücke sind vier Antwortmöglichkeiten vorgegeben, die du dir genau durchlesen solltest. Wenn du dich für eine Antwort entschieden hast, überprüfe deine Wahl auch noch einmal anhand des Ausschlussverfahrens. Für jede richtige Antwort bekommst du einen Punkt.*

1.		2.		3.		4.	
☑	herself	☐	easily	☑	teaching	☐	somebody
☐	her	☐	easy	☐	taught	☑	anyone
☐	she	☑	simply	☐	going to teach	☐	anything
☐	hers	☐	simple	☐	will teach	☐	someone

5.		6.		7.		8.	
☑	might be	☐	Where	☐	becomes	☐	healthiest
☐	have to be	☐	How	☐	mixes	☑	healthily
☐	are able to	☐	What	☑	turns	☐	health
☐	might	☑	Why	☐	stays	☐	healthy

9.		10.		11.		12.	
☐	has been	☑	having fun	☐	by	☑	already
☐	will be	☐	being funny	☐	on	☐	still
☐	had been	☐	have fun	☑	at	☐	ever
☑	would be	☐	be funny	☐	of	☐	never

*✏ **Hinweise:***

zu 1: *Nur das Reflexivpronomen* herself *ist richtig, da die Lehrerin sich selbst beschreibt.*

zu 2: *Dass ein Adverb verlangt wird, kannst du an der Wortstellung erkennen (das Adjektiv würde vor dem Nomen stehen:* a simple job). Easily *bedeutet, dass etwas einfach, leicht zu tun ist,* simply *bedeutet „einfach (nur)" und ist daher hier passend.*

zu 3: *Das Verb* involve *zieht entweder ein Nomen oder eine -ing-Form nach sich, daher kann hier nur* teaching *stehen.*

zu 4: *Es geht um Personen, also fällt* anything *weg. Da hier gemeint ist, dass* alle *Schülerinnen und Schüler chemische Berufe ergreifen können, musst du* anyone *wählen –* somebody/someone *bedeutet „(irgend-)jemand".*

zu 5: *Hier ist gemeint: Die Schülerinnen und Schüler* könnten *verunsichert sein.* Have to be initimidated *würde bedeuten „müssen verunsichert sein" und* are able to be intimidated *„können verunsichert sein". Da* might *immer mit Infinitiv steht, ist* might *be die gesuchte Lösung.*

zu 6: *Das Fragewort „Why" ist inhaltlich das einzige Fragewort, das Sinn ergibt; denn man kann am Satzanfang des Antwortsatzes* (Because) *erkennen, dass hier „Why" stehen muss.*

zu 7: turn to *bedeutet „werden zu, sich verwandeln in". Die anderen drei Verben werden nicht mit* to *kombiniert und ergeben auch inhaltlich keinen Sinn.*

zu 8: *Hier steht ein Adverb, das das Verb* eat *näher beschreibt und beantwortet,* wie *sich die Schülerinnen und Schüler ernähren (gesund). Vielleicht hast du auch schon die Wendung* eat healthy *gehört, die immer häufiger vorkommt. Grammatikalisch richtig ist aber nur* healthily.

zu 9: *Hier liegt ein If-Satz Typ II vor, den du am* if *und am „simple past" im Nebensatz erkennst. Bei Typ II steht im Hauptsatz* would + Infinitiv.

zu 10: *Nach* interested in *steht die -ing-Form. In diesem Satz geht es darum, Spaß zu haben und nicht darum, lustig zu sein, deshalb passt hier nur* having fun.

zu 11: *Das Wort* school *wird normalerweise mit den Präpositionen* at *oder* in *verwendet, wenn „in der Schule" gemeint ist. Da* in *nicht zur Auswahl steht, kann nur* at *stimmen.*

zu 12: *In diese Lücke passt inhaltlich nur* already *(„schon").*

D Text Production

Hinweis: Im letzten Teil der Prüfung, der Textproduktion, kannst du zwischen zwei Aufgaben wählen. Dieser Teil wird mit 25 Punkten, also einem Viertel der Gesamt-punktzahl, gewertet. Du kannst entscheiden, ob du eine Geschichte zu einem vorgege-benen Bild oder einen Artikel für deine Schülerzeitung (hier: Thema „Klassenzimmer-Wettbewerb") schreiben möchtest. Du sollst in deinem Text auf mindestens vier der fünf vorgegebenen Aspekte bzw. Fragen eingehen und ungefähr 150 Wörter schrei-ben. Die hier abgedruckten Lösungsvorschläge sind etwas länger, um dir verschie-dene Ideen zu geben. Neben den Punkten für Inhalt (10 Punkte), Grammatik (5 Punkte) und Wortschatz (5 Punkte) gibt es weitere 5 Punkte für die Organisation deines Textes. Achte deshalb beim Schreiben darauf, dass dein Text klar strukturiert ist, d. h., es muss ein „roter Faden" durch Einleitung, Hauptteil und Schluss zu er-kennen sein. Dein Text sollte darüber hinaus über Absätze eine äußerliche Struktur erhalten. Zähle abschließend die Wörter. Du darfst die Wortzahl überschreiten, wenn dein Text durchgehend sinnvoll ist und es zu keinen Wiederholungen kommt.

What is the story behind the picture?

Hinweis: Du kannst deiner Fantasie freien Lauf lassen und deine Lösung kann auch dann gut sein, wenn sie andere inhaltliche Schwerpunkte setzt als der Lösungs-vorschlag. Achte aber in jedem Fall darauf, mindestens vier der vorgegebenen As-pekte abzudecken und dir das Bild genau anzuschauen, damit dein Text plausibel ist.

The boy in this picture is my big brother Jimmy. He is my hero, and this is his heroic story.

Yesterday evening, as usual, I was preparing food for my little cat Lily. However, I could not find her! I called her and looked for her in every single corner she loves hiding but she was not there. I panicked and was scared something could have hap-pened to her. As my parents had gone out to the theatre, I called Jimmy in a panic.

You see, he does everything for his little sister: he was at a party with his classmates, but he left to help me find Lily.

Together, we continued to look for Lily everywhere. When it was late and we had almost given up, Jimmy suddenly heard a noise coming from the top of a tree. He pointed his torchlight at the branches and there she was! On the highest of all the trees. Jimmy, who knows no fear, climbed up the tree and rescued her. I was so happy to have her back!

After that Jimmy was so exhausted that he fell asleep right on the sofa and little Lily comforted him.

196 words

Glamour and Glory

Hinweis: Du sollst beschreiben, wie deine Klasse den Schulwettbewerb zum coolsten Klassenzimmer gewann. Überlege dir plausible Antworten auf mindestens vier der Fragen und schreibe dann deinen Artikel für die Schülerzeitung.

Our head teacher's idea to hold a competition on the coolest classroom was great – you all know how boring most of our classrooms looked before the competition … That's why we students from 10 B wanted to take part right away. We collected ideas and chose the best one: A jungle classroom. Some of our classmates are real artists and talented in painting. So we decided to colour the walls and paint a scene out of the jungle on it, with palm trees, tigers, monkeys and parrots.

In addition, the other pupils planned and organized the rest of the decoration. They collected money, built huge paper palm trees and even bought some plants that are easy to handle and look like plants you find in the jungle.

The result is worth seeing! We have the coolest classroom ever because it looks so real. Everytime I go in I feel like I might meet Mowgli around the corner … It is much more fun to learn here now and we will spend the prize money on a trip to a fun park which has got a jungle theme. *187 words*

A Listening Comprehension

Hinweis: Der Hörverstehensteil der Abschlussprüfung 2020 besteht aus drei Teilen. Alle Texte werden zweimal vorgespielt. Du kannst während des Abspielens jederzeit mit deinen Eintragungen beginnen. Im ersten Teil hörst du zwei Nachrichten, der zweite Teil ist eine Umfrage und der dritte Teil ist ein Interview.

Part One

Hinweis: Du hast am Anfang 20 Sekunden Zeit, dir die Aussagen zu „News Item 1" durchzulesen. Während des ersten Hörens kannst du mit Bleistift mögliche Antworten ankreuzen, deine endgültigen Antworten musst du dann aber mit Füller oder Kugelschreiber festhalten. Für jede richtige Antwort erhältst du einen Punkt. Wenn du bei einer Teilaufgabe mehrere Antworten ankreuzt, erhältst du keinen Punkt.

Im ersten „News Item" geht es um eine Zwölfjährige mit dem Spitznamen „Rapunzel", den sie wegen ihrer sehr langen Haare hat. Du musst beantworten, wie lang ihr Haar ist (a), wie sie im Alltag mit ihren Haaren umgeht (b), wie ihre Familie auf die Situation reagiert (c) und warum „Rapunzel" nicht schwimmen gehen kann (d).

Vor „News Item 2" hast du noch einmal 20 Sekunden Zeit, die Aufgaben zu lesen. Es geht um einen als Big Ben verkleideten Läufer. Du musst herausfinden, was die Rekordzeit eines als Wahrzeichen verkleideten Läufers ist (a), warum Lukas Bates den Marathon nicht beenden konnte (b), was am Ende geschah (c) und wo der Weltrekord des schnellsten als Wahrzeichen verkleideten Marathonläufers aufgestellt wurde (d).

News Item 1

a) Natasha's hair is
- [ ] longer than she is.
- [✓] shorter than she is.
- [ ] the same length as she is.

Hinweis: "she is just two centimetres taller than the length of her beautiful, thick brown hair." (Z. 6–8)

b) Natasha
- [ ] washes her hair every day.
- [ ] brushes her hair for one and a half hours every week.
- [✓] has to hold her hair when walking.

Hinweis: "She has to carry it when she walks" (Z. 10/11)

c) Her family
- [ ] call her Rapunzel.
- [ ] love her hair.
- [✓] suffer because of her hair.

🖋 **Hinweis:** *"Natasha's family cannot switch on the fan because her hair gets caught in it. The heat in the house is a real problem for them all." (Z. 12–15)*

d) Natasha can't go swimming because
- [ ] her hair gets in the way.
- [✓] the saltwater ruins her hair.
- [ ] it takes hours to dry her hair.

🖋 **Hinweis:** *"because the seawater damages her hair" (Z. 20/21)*

News Item 2

a) The fastest time for a runner dressed as a landmark is
- [ ] 3 hours 54 minutes.
- [✓] 3 hours 34 minutes.
- [ ] 2 hours 59 minutes.

🖋 **Hinweis:** *"The current record stands at three hours and 34 minutes." (Z. 6/7)*

b) Marathon runner Lukas Bates could not finish the race because
- [✓] of his costume.
- [ ] of Big Ben.
- [ ] of a volunteer.

🖋 **Hinweis:** *"the 30-year-old was unable to fit under the race clock at the finishing line because the top of his Big Ben costume was too tall." (Z. 9–12)*

c) In the end, Lukas
- [ ] ran across the finishing line.
- [ ] was helped by a race volunteer.
- [✓] crawled over the line.

🖋 **Hinweis:** *"Lukas finally crossed over the line on his hands and knees." (Z. 14/15)*

d) The world record for the fastest marathon time dressed as a landmark was set in
- [✓] Berlin.
- [ ] Lübeck.
- [ ] London.

🖋 **Hinweis:** *"The record for the fastest marathon time dressed as a landmark, […] was set by Richard Mietz at the Berlin Marathon" (Z. 18–21)*

Part Two

✎ *Hinweis: Teil 2 ist eine Umfrage, in der ein Reporter sieben Personen zum Thema „Insekten essen" befragt. Die Aussagen sind in Sprechblasen vorgegeben und du musst sie den richtigen Personen zuordnen. Für jede richtige Zuordnung bekommst du einen Punkt. Beachte, dass es sieben Personen, aber acht Aussagen gibt, eine Aussage bleibt also übrig.*
Zum Lesen der Aussagen hast du 40 Sekunden Zeit. Unterstreiche Schlüsselwörter in den Sprechblasen, auf die du dich während des Zuhörens konzentrieren kannst.

Julie	David	Mia	Archie	Katy	Dora	Jenna
C	H	F	E	B	A	D

✎ *Hinweise:*
zu Julie: "Insects are a regular part of the diet in many countries in Central and South America, Africa and Asia." (Z. 11–14)
zu David: "insects are really good for you. For example, a 100-gramme portion of red ants contains about 14 grammes of protein as well as a lot of iron. Many other insects are a great source of nutrients as well." (Z. 20–24)
zu Mia: "Farming insects […] produces between 10 and 80 times less methane gas than farming other animals." (Z. 29–31)
zu Archie: "Many insects feed on rotting food, dead animals and human waste, which is full of bacteria, and unfortunately, many insect farms in Asia don't follow high hygienic standards and this results in illness." (Z. 37–41)
zu Katy: "Did you know that insect farms are not as difficult to operate as cattle farms?" (Z. 42–44)
zu Dora: "A kilogramme of feed given to a cricket will produce twelve times more protein than the same amount given to cattle" (Z. 54–57)
zu Jenna: "we actually already eat more insects than you think." (Z. 62/63)

Part Three

✎ *Hinweis: Hier hörst du ein Interview mit dem Schwimmer Ross Edgley, der als erste Person rund um Großbritannien geschwommen ist.*
Lies die Aufgabenstellung genau durch und ergänze die gesuchten Informationen in der Tabelle. Du sollst jeweils nur eine Information angeben; machst du mehrere Angaben und ist eine davon falsch, erhältst du keinen Punkt. Pro Tabellenfeld kannst du einen Punkt erreichen. Bei sprachlichen Fehlern werden dir keine Punkte abgezogen, solange der Inhalt verständlich und korrekt ist. Stichpunkte reichen aus, Zahlen musst du nicht ausschreiben.

(1) how far Ross swam	**2,885 km / 2,885 kilometres / around the coast of Great Britain**
(2) one of Ross' other world records	• **longest rope climb** • **climbing 8,800 metres up a rope** • **running a marathon pulling a (small) car**
(3) when Ross started his swim	**1st June**
(4) one reason why the swim took longer	• **(The) weather was unpredictable.** • **(There were) high waves / strong currents.** • **(The) cold slowed him down.**
(5) swimming routine	**(He) swam for six hours and slept six hours.**
(6) where Ross slept	**on the (support) boat**
(7) one difficulty Ross experienced	• **jellyfish stings** • **(open) wounds** • **(He) damaged (the muscles in) his shoulder.**
(8) what food he ate to get energy (one detail)	• **pizza** • **pasta** • **rice pudding** • **bananas**
(9) how he felt when he arrived back in Margate	**(He was really) emotional. / (He) started to cry. / (He felt) relieved.**
(10) current plans (one detail)	**(He wants to)** • **stay warm and dry.** • **learn to use his feet again for walking.** • **adapt to normal life (again).** • **wait for the next adventure.**

Hinweise:

zu 1: *"Ross, you swam 2,885 kilometres around the coast of Great Britain."* *(Z. 6/7)*

zu 2: *"You have two other world records. You hold the record for the longest rope climb. You climbed 8,800 metres in 19 hours. You have run a marathon pulling a small car." (Z. 12–15)*

zu 3: *"I left Margate [...] on the 1st of June" (Z. 23/24)*

zu 4: *"the weather was unpredictable." (Z. 28)/ "There were days when the waves were really high." (Z. 28/29)/ "There were strong currents" (Z. 30)/ "the cold slowed me down" (Z. 31)*
<u>Beachte</u>: *Für die Antworten "weather" oder "cold" oder "water" wird kein Punkt vergeben. Deine Antwort muss immer ein Nomen und ein dazugehöriges Merkmal enthalten, z. B. "bad weather" oder "cold water".*
zu 5: *"I swam for six hours and then slept for six hours." (Z. 33/34)*
zu 6: *"I slept on the support boat." (Z. 40/41)*
zu 7: *"I was stung 37 times by jellyfish." (Z. 47/48)/ "I also had open wounds on my body" (Z. 48)/ "I damaged the muscles in my shoulder." (Z. 49/50)*
zu 8: *"Pizza, pasta, rice pudding […] bananas" (Z. 55)*
<u>Beachte</u>: *Für die Antworten "proteins" oder "energy drinks" werden keine Punkte vergeben, da nach konkreten Nahrungsmitteln gefragt ist.*
zu 9: *"I was really emotional." (Z. 60); "I had to put my goggles back on because I was starting to cry." (Z. 63–65)*
zu 10: *"I just want to stay warm and dry" (Z. 68)/ "I have to learn to use my feet again for walking." (Z. 69/70)/ "I […] just need to adapt to normal life again." (Z. 70/71)*
<u>Beachte</u>: *Für die alleinigen Antworten "learn walking" oder "enjoy the moment" werden keine Punkte vergeben.*

B Reading Comprehension

1. Influence of social media on teens

Hinweis: Hier musst du die Überschriften (A–G) den Abschnitten eines Textes (1–5) zuordnen. Es gibt sieben Überschriften, aber nur fünf Textabschnitte, zwei Überschriften bleiben also übrig. Für jede richtige Zuordnung bekommst du einen Punkt. Lies die Textabschnitte durch und suche nach Schlüsselwörtern, die du in den Überschriften wiederfindest. Vielleicht findest du auch Synonyme oder Umschreibungen wieder. Achte bei der Zuordnung darauf, dass die Überschrift alle Aspekte des Textabschnittes berücksichtigt.

part of the text	❶	❷	❸	❹	❺
heading	F	A	G	D	E

Hinweise:
zu 1: Im ersten Textabschnitt wird die wachsende Sorge vieler Eltern beschrieben, dass Social-Media-Seiten wie Instagram und Facebook schlecht für ihre Kinder sein könnten.

zu 2: Hier geht es um Studien zu den Auswirkungen sozialer Medien auf junge Menschen. Die Studienergebnisse zeigen, dass die Nutzung sozialer Medien sowohl negative Folgen haben kann als auch positive, sie sind also „mixed" und stehen im Widerspruch zueinander.

zu 3: Textabschnitt 3 verweist auf die negativen Folgen des Social-Media-Gebrauchs: Jugendliche, die sehr häufig soziale Netzwerke nutzen, neigen zu Depressionen und Stimmungsschwankungen.

zu 4: Textabschnitt 4 zeigt auf, dass vor allem junge Frauen sich mit digital bearbeiteten Bildern in sozialen Netzwerken vergleichen und sich dadurch oft hässlich oder dick fühlen. Dies kann zu Essstörungen führen.

zu 5: Hier wird erklärt, dass von den Jugendlichen, die sehr viele Videospiele machen, diejeinigen seltener psychische Probleme bekommen, die über soziale Netzwerke Freundschaften pflegen.

2. **Why Scotland loves haggis**

Hinweis: Bei dieser Multiple-Choice-Aufgabe musst du die vorgegebenen Satzanfänge vervollständigen. Es ist immer nur eine Antwort richtig. Die Aufgaben sind in der Regel chronologisch angeordnet, d. h. die Antwort zur ersten Aufgabe findest du zu Beginn des Textes, die zur nächsten etwas weiter unten im Text usw. Lies dir den Text einmal komplett durch, bevor du mit dem Beantworten der Fragen beginnst. Wenn du beim ersten Lesen nicht alles verstehst, lass dich nicht verunsichern. Wenn du dich intensiver mit den einzelnen Abschnitten beschäftigst, kannst du vieles aus dem Zusammenhang erschließen. Markiere zuerst Schlüsselwörter in dem Satz, den du vervollständigen musst, und dann in dazugehörigen Stellen im Text, die dir die Antwort verraten. So findest du die entsprechenden Textstellen schnell wieder, wenn du deine Lösungen am Ende noch einmal überprüfst.

a) In the past, especially poorer people needed to
- ☐ preserve their internal organs.
- ☐ salt and dry their haggis.
- ☐ eat their haggis at once.
- ☑ use almost all parts of an animal.

Hinweis: "In those days it was essential for poorer people to use as much of an animal as possible." (Z. 1/2)

b) Haggis is cooked
- ☐ with whisky.
- ☐ in a balloon.
- ☑ gently.
- ☐ in a dish.

E 2020-6

🖋 **Hinweis:** *"cooked slowly for two or three hours at a low temperature."*
(Z. 8/9)

c) Originally, haggis was eaten
   ☑ by travellers.
   ☐ by Robert Burns.
   ☐ out of tins.
   ☐ in restaurants.

   🖋 **Hinweis:** *"In its early days, haggis served as a hearty meal for those on the move across Scotland" (Z. 12)*

d) Today, you can buy this traditional dish
   ☐ only on Burns Night.
   ☐ only in tins.
   ☑ at any time.
   ☐ only in fast-food shops.

   🖋 **Hinweis:** *"haggis is still eaten year-round – you can even buy it in tins or from fast food shops." (Z. 16/17)*

e) Robert Burns was a Scottish
   ☐ whisky-maker.
   ☐ trader.
   ☑ writer.
   ☐ cook.

   🖋 **Hinweis:** *"Scotland's national poet, Robert Burns" (Z. 19)*

f) Burns night was first celebrated
   ☑ five years after Burns had died.
   ☐ in 1759.
   ☐ on January 25th.
   ☐ on Robert Burns' birthday.

   🖋 **Hinweis:** *"The first Burns Night was celebrated in 1801 […] when a group of his friends came together […] to celebrate his life and achievements on the fifth anniversary of the poet's death" (Z. 20–22)*

g) On Burns Night, haggis is normally served with
   ☐ soup.
   ☑ vegetables.
   ☐ meat.
   ☐ oats.

   🖋 **Hinweis:** *"It is traditionally served with 'neeps and tatties' – turnip and potato" (Z. 26)*

h) Cooks sometimes pour whisky

☐ into the soup.
☑ into the sauce.
☐ over the haggis.
☐ onto the plates.

Hinweis: "Cooks can make a whisky-based sauce to serve with the haggis" (Z. 29/30)

i) Burns Night traditionally starts with

☑ Scottish music.
☐ Scottish history.
☐ a glass of whisky.
☐ a reading of the recipe.

Hinweis: "The feast tradtionally begins with a bagpiper playing while haggis is carried to the table." (Z. 34/35)

k) "Auld Lang Syne" is usually sung

☐ at the beginning of the evening.
☑ at the end of the evening.
☐ when the haggis arrives.
☐ before reading a poem.

Hinweis: "The host closes the evening by inviting guests to stand and sing 'Auld Lang Syne'". (Z. 36)

3. Take your seats, everyone

Hinweis: Ganz am Anfang solltest du den Romanauszug einmal komplett durchlesen, damit du weißt, wovon er handelt. Danach liest du am besten die Fragen, damit du beim zweiten Lesen des Textes die Stellen, die die Antworten verraten, markieren kannst. Du musst nicht in vollständigen Sätzen antworten. Für sprachliche Fehler werden dir keine Punkte angezogen, sofern deine Antwort verständlich und inhaltlich richtig ist.

a) – huge
   – sparkly chandeliers
   – red velvet walls
   – rows of cushioned seats
   – giant stage
   – wide aisle

Hinweis: "The auditorium was huge inside. Big sparkly chandeliers. Red velvet walls. Rows and rows and rows of cushioned seats leading up to the giant stage. We walked down the wide aisle" (Z. 3–5)

b) (They are in) fifth grade.

Hinweis: "*We walked down the wide aisle and followed the signs to the fifth-grade staging area*" (Z. 5/6)

c) (They should sit) alphabetically.

Hinweis: " '*you're sitting alphabetically.* ' " (Z. 8)

d) He tells her that she looks awesome.

Hinweis: " '*Wow, Summer, you look awesome* ' " (Z. 13).
<u>*Beachte:*</u> *Für eine Antwort in falscher Perspektive, z. B.* "<u>I</u> *tell <u>her</u>", wird kein Punkt vergeben.*

e) Because of the program./Summer's mom dozed off last year./Mr. Jansen's speeches always go on forever/Because of Mr. Jansen's speech.

Hinweis: " '*Oh man, look at this program* ' [...] '*We're going to be here all freakin' day.* ' " (Z. 17/18)/ " '*Because Mr. Jansen's speeches go on forever* ' " (Z. 19)./ " '*My mom said she actually dozed off when he spoke last year* ' " (Z. 21)

f) She is annoyed that nobody is listening./The students don't sit down./The students forget that they are sitting in alphabetical order./They have a lot to get through.

Hinweis: "*Ms. Rubin started yelling louder now, like she was getting annoyed that nobody was listening.* '*We have a lot to get through, so take your seats. Don't forget that you're sitting in alphabetical order!* ' " (Z. 25–27)

g) He looks at Ms. Rubin blankly./He says, "I am?"/He looks confused./He looks like he has just played a joke on someone.

Hinweis: "*Jack looked at her blankly.*" (Z. 35)/ " '*I am?* ' " (Z. 36)/ "*a mixture of looking completly confused and looking like he's just played a joke on someone*" (Z. 36/37)

h) He finds Summer very attractive and doesn't want to show it.

Hinweis: Die Antwort auf diese Frage steht nicht direkt im Text. August ist, wie man in der Einleitung erfährt, ein einger Freund von Jack. Er bemerkt aber erst, dass Jack in Summer verliebt ist, als Jack zu Summer sagt, dass sie „okay" aussieht (vgl. Z. 14), obwohl sie richtig gut aussieht, wie August kurz zuvor sagt (vgl. Z. 13). Später gibt Jack das August gegenüber auch zu (vgl. Z. 31). Dass Jack sich nicht traut, offen zu sagen, wie hübsch er Summer findet, deutet darauf hin, dass er in sie verliebt ist, es ihr aber nicht zeigen möchte.
<u>*Beachte:*</u> *Für die alleinige Antwort* "He has a crush on her" *wird kein Punkt vergeben. Aus deiner Antwort muss auch hervorgehen, dass Jack diesen „crush" für sich behalten möchte.*

i) (He means/is referring to) the very clever students/students who are very intelligent/the best students/students who get good marks.

Hinweis: brainiac *heißt übersetzt etwa „Intelligenzbestie" oder „Super-hirn". Du kannst dir die Bedeutung des Wortes erschließen, da das Wort* brain, *also „Gehirn", darin enthalten ist. Es handelt sich also um Schülerinnen und Schüler, die besonders intelligent sind und dafür ausgezeichnet werden.*
Beachte: Für die Antwort "students who get medals" *wird kein Punkt verge-ben, da sie zu allgemein ist. Aus deiner Antwort muss hervorgehen, dass es sich um besonders intelligente/begabte/clevere/hervorragende Schülerinnen und Schüler handelt.*

C Use of Language

1. Mediation – The switched RV

Hinweis: Die Mediation ist in zwei Teile gegliedert. Im ersten Teil sollst du die wichtigsten Fakten aus der englischen E-Mail eines Wohnmobilvermieters an dei-nen Onkel wiedergeben. Du kannst Textstellen in der E-Mail markieren und bei Bedarf wichtige Ausdrücke in deinem Wörterbuch nachschlagen.

Im zweiten Teil der Mediation bittet dich dein Onkel, den Wohnmobilvermieter anzurufen. Auf dieses Gespräch bereitest du dich vor, indem du das Hauptanliegen auf Englisch formulierst und anschließend vier weitere wichtige Informationen bzw. Fragen, die du weitergeben sollst, aufschreibst.

Achte darauf, die richtige Perspektive einzunehmen, also z. B. im zweiten Teil in der 3. Person Singular („My uncle"/„He") zu sprechen und nicht in der Ich-Per-spektive. Wenn du eine falsche Perspektive einnimmst (egal ob einmal oder mehr-fach), wird dir von der Gesamtpunktzahl der Mediation einmalig ein Punkt abge-zogen. Gibst du Antworten in der falschen Sprache, bekommst du keinen Punkt. Wenn du statt „Wohnmobil" den englischen Begriff „RV" verwendest, ist das auch in Ordnung und gibt einen Punkt.

Zwei Hauptanliegen:
– Der Vermieter teilt mit, dass das (gebuchte) (Standard-)Wohnmobil nicht zur Verfügung steht.
– Der Vermieter bietet als Ersatz ein kleineres/Compact Wohnmobil an./Der Vermieter bietet einen Ersatz/ein anderes Wohnmobil an.

Hinweis: Für die Aussage „Der Vermieter ist ausgebucht" wird kein Punkt ver-geben, da dabei die für deinen Onkel wichtige Information fehlt, dass er das ei-gentlich gebuchte Wohnmobil nicht nutzen kann.

Fünf weitere wichtige Informationen:
– Drei Personen können darin/im kleineren Wohnmobil schlafen./Es passen drei Passagiere in das (kleinere) Wohnmobil.
– (Der) Tisch lässt sich in (ein) Bett verwandeln.

- (Der) Raum über der Fahrerkabine lässt sich in (ein) Doppelbett verwandeln/zu einem Doppelbett ausziehen/umbauen.
- (Das kleinere) Wohnmobil (ist) nur 2,3 Meter breit.
- (Das kleinere) Wohnmobil (ist) besser für Wohnmobil-Anfänger geeignet.
- (Das) Fahren auf engen Straßen ist einfacher/sicherer.
- einfacheres Parken/Das Parken ist (mit dem kleineren Wohnmobil) einfacher.
- 300 Freimeilen
- Küchenutensilien (normalerweise $ 110) kostenlos./Man spart 110 Dollar.
- Du sollst schnell antworten, da die Wohnmobilvermietung viele Anfragen für diesen Zeitraum hat.
- Man kann bei der Vermietung anrufen oder eine E-Mail schreiben.

Hinweis: Die Antwort „300 freie Kilometer" statt „300 Freimeilen" ergibt keinen Punkt. Für „Küchen-Kit" statt „Küchenutensilien" wird kein Punkt vergeben.

Hauptanliegen:
My uncle will accept the offer/book the Compact RV.

Vier weitere wichtige Informationen oder Fragen:
- My uncle is not happy about the smaller RV.
- How much work is it to prepare/make up the beds?
- My uncle is 1.95 metres tall – is the RV high enough for him to stand comfortably?
- Is the bathroom big enough for a tall person to shower comfortably?
- Does this RV use less gas?/Will the gas cost less?/What are the fuel costs?

Hinweis: Die Hauptaussage "My uncle has many questions about the RV" ergibt keinen Punkt.

2. **Words and structures – Police museum[1]**

Hinweis: Diese Aufgabe überprüft deine Kenntnisse in Wortschatz und Grammatik in Form eines Lückentextes. Lies den Text gut durch und wähle aus der Box das passende Wort für die jeweilige Lücke aus. Beachte, dass jedes Wort nur einmal verwendet werden darf und dass in der Box mehr Wörter stehen, als es im Text Lücken gibt. Du erhältst keinen Punkt, wenn du ein Wort falsch abschreibst oder es fälschlicherweise mit einem Großbuchstaben am Anfang schreibst.

Police shows on TV are filled with high-speed car chases and crimes solved quickly – within a few (1) **minutes**. But that is not a typical day for a real-life police officer. At the new National Law Enforcement Museum in Washington, interactive (2) **displays** invite visitors to use their (3) **senses** of sight, hearing, touch and smell.

In that way, they can learn about the way police officers, detectives and forensic scientists do (4) **their** work.

Visitors can discover how footprints and DNA help solve crimes. They can also sit in a real police car that officers (5) **used** on the streets. There, the visitors can learn (6) **about** the meaning of different emergency light patterns and sirens.

Visitors will (7) **quickly** learn that crime-solving is a team effort, not only within one police department, but among many law enforcement agencies across the country. For example, six agencies worked together on a national park graffiti case. There is also a video of how dogs (8) **are trained** before they join the so-called K-9 units, where dogs are partners of police officers. Visitors learn which dogs are good for tracking the bad guys and which dogs are better (9) **at** sniffing out drugs.

Visitors (10) **who** are at least twelve years old can try the same training scenarios and equipment used in professional law enforcement classes. Short videos test the (11) **participants'** abilities to observe accurately and think quickly before reacting. The exercises give an understanding of what officers face on a daily basis. Because every community is different, the museum shows (12) **how** the needs and challenges of different communities are being addressed. There are programs to minimize problems and reduce (13) **crime**, while increasing trust between residents and police.

Ann Cameron Siegal: New museum lets visitors walk in the shoes of a police officer, *Washington Post* vom 28. 11. 2018, https://www.washingtonpost.com/lifestyle/kidspost/a-look-into-the-new-national-law-enforce ment-museum/2018/11/27/f4928072-f1ae-11e8-aeea-b85fd44449f5_story.html (adaptiert), From The Washington Post. © 2018 The Washington Post. All rights reserved. Used under license.

1 Der Originaltext des Artikels aus der *Washington Post* lautet:

Police shows on TV are filled with high-speed car chases and crimes solved in a matter of minutes. But that's not a typical day for a real-life police officer. To get a more accurate picture, head to the new National Law Enforcement Museum in Washington. Interactive exhibits there invite visitors to use their senses of sight, hearing, touch and smell in gathering information the way police, detectives and forensic scientists do.

Explore how footprints and DNA, or genetic material, help solve crimes. Sit in an actual police cruiser as you learn the meaning of different emergency light patterns and sirens.

"It's a walk-in-their-shoes experience," said Julie Bell, the museum's manager of school programs. Let's look at a few exhibits.

The Web of Law Enforcement: You'll quickly learn that crime- solving is a team effort, not only within one department, but among agencies across the country. The FBI, Secret Service, Coast Guard and Postal […] Inspection Service are just some of the law enforcement groups helping local police when needed. For example, six agencies worked together on a national park graffiti case.

K-9 units: See a video of how dogs are trained to join K-9 units. Test your ability to smell and identify various scents. Learn which breeds are better at tracking the bad guys while others are better at sniffing out drugs. Why are Chihuahuas better at some tasks than German shepherds?

The Training Simulator: Those age 12 and older can try the same training scenarios and equipment used in professional law enforcement classes in which police try to resolve difficult situations. Short videos, based on real police encounters, test participants' abilities to observe accurately and think quickly before reacting.

The exercises give an understanding of what officers face on a daily basis.

"Many kids first think it's like a video game," said Alan Davis, an educator and retired New York police officer. "They soon realize that real-life split-second decision-making isn't easy, and they freeze. For real police, there are no second chances." […]

Five Communities (current programs): Every community is different. Learn how the needs and challenges of five communities are being addressed. These communities' goals are to develop programs to minimize problems and reduce crime, while increasing trust between residents and police. What might work in your neighborhood? There's a place for visitors to share their thoughts.

As Luther Reynolds, police chief in Charleston, South Carolina, told the museum, "There is no department in this country that doesn't have the room to get better."

Hinweise:

zu 1: Hier fehlt ein Nomen im Plural. Die Formulierung within a few *(„innerhalb weniger") zeigt, dass hier nur* minutes *passt.*

zu 2: Auch in diese Lücke muss ein Nomen gesetzt werden, und weil kein Artikel dabei steht, muss es wieder im Plural stehen. Inhaltlich kann die Lücke nur mit dem Wort displays *(→ „interaktive Darstellungen") gefüllt werden.*

zu 3: Daraus, dass nach dem gesuchten Wort sight, hearing, touch and smell *(Sehen, Hören, Fühlen und Riechen) steht, kannst du schließen, dass es sich um die* Sinne *(senses) handelt.*

zu 4: In dieser Lücke fehlt ein passender Begleiter zum Nomen work. *Der einzige Begleiter im grauen Kasten – und damit die richtige Lösung – ist der Possessivbegleiter* their *(→ „ihre Arbeit").*

zu 5: Das Wort real *verrät dir, dass es sich um ein echtes (aber ausrangiertes) Polizeiauto handelt, das früher wirklich verwendet wurde. Daher kommt nur die Verbform* used *infrage.*

zu 6: Hier fehlt eine Präposition, und das Verb learn *wird normalerweise mit der Präposition* about *verwendet, wenn „etwas lernen" gemeint ist.*

zu 7: Dass ein Adverb verlangt wird, kannst du an der Wortstellung erkennen (ein Adjektiv würde vor dem Nomen stehen, z. B. quick visitors). *Das fehlende Adverb beschreibt das Verb* learn *näher. Da* quickly *„schnell, rasch" bedeutet, ist es hier passend.*

zu 8: Hier passt nur die Passivform are trained, *denn es wird ein Verb im Präsens benötigt, wie du an der folgenden Verbform* join *(ebenfalls Präsens) erkennen kannst.*

zu 9: Der Ausdruck to be good/bad/better *(„in etwas gut/schlecht/besser sein") wird im Englischen immer mit der Präposition* at *benutzt.*

zu 10: Die Besucher (visitors) *werden hier durch einen Relativsatz näher beschrieben. Außer* whose, *das besitzanzeigend ist und daher hier nicht passt, ist* who *das einzige Relativpronomen im grauen Kasten; da* who *bei Personen verwendet wird, ist es die richtige Lösung.*

zu 11: Es wird ein Nomen im Genitiv benötigt (wessen Fähigkeiten? → die Fähigkeiten der Teilnehmenden). Da das Wort participants' *die einzige Genitivform in der Box ist, ist es die richtige Lösung.*
Beachte: Die Lösungen participant's *und* participant *ergeben keinen Punkt.*

zu 12: Das Adverb how *ist inhaltlich das einzige Wort, das Sinn ergibt. Der Ausdruck* to show how *bedeutet „zeigen, wie".*

zu 13: Hier kannst du mit dem Ausschlussverfahren viel erreichen: Da es sich um etwas handelt, das reduziert werden soll, muss es etwas Negatives sein. Außerdem brauchst du ein Nomen. Da criminal („Verbrecher*in") nicht passt, kann hier nur crime stehen.

D Text Production

Hinweis: Im letzten Teil der Abschlussprüfung, der Textproduktion, hast du die Wahl zwischen zwei Aufgaben. Bei der Textproduktion kannst du 25 Punkte, also ein Viertel der Gesamtpunktzahl, erreichen. Du kannst entscheiden, ob du einen Text zu dem vorgegebenen Bild oder einen Text für einen Schreibwettbewerb zum Thema „Die Bedeutung des Reisens" schreiben möchtest.

Bei beiden Themen solltest du ungefähr 150 Wörter schreiben und in deinem Text mindestens vier der fünf vorgegebenen Fragen bearbeiten.

Neben den Punkten für Inhalt (10 Punkte), Grammatik (5 Punkte) und Wortschatz (5 Punkte) gibt es weitere 5 Punkte für die Organisation deines Textes. Achte deshalb darauf, dass dein Text klar strukturiert ist, d. h., es muss ein „roter Faden" durch Einleitung, Hauptteil und Schluss zu erkennen sein. Dein Text sollte darüber hinaus durch Absätze strukturiert sein. Im Lösungsvorschlag stehen als Hilfe bei jedem Absatz am Rand kurze Stichpunkte zur Orientierung. Auch wenn du andere Formulierungen oder Argumente verwendet hast, kannst du so vergleichen, ob du die wichtigen Aspekte bedacht und deinen Text gut strukturiert hast.

Zähle die Wörter, wenn du mit dem Schreiben fertig bist. Wenn dein Text durchgehend sinnvoll ist und es zu keinen Wiederholungen kommt, darfst du auch mehr als 150 Wörter schreiben. Die Lösungsvorschläge sind bewusst etwas länger, damit du Anregungen für die inhaltliche Ausgestaltung und für gute Formulierungen erhältst.

What is the story behind the picture?

Hinweis: Schau dir das Bild genau an und überlege, was die beiden Jungen wohl machen und wo sie sich befinden könnten. Deiner Kreativität sind keine Grenzen gesetzt, solange deine Gedanken nachvollziehbar sind und du vier der fünf vorgegebenen Punkte berücksichtigst.

So many people say that teenagers are just living for their mobiles nowadays. As a teen, I am annoyed by that and do not think it is true. But my experience yesterday showed me that sometimes it can be true and now I understand better why many parents do not like it if their children use their smartphones so much.   Einleitung

In the afternoon I went shopping and while I was walking along the street, I saw two of my friends, Tim and Leo, sitting on the pavement. However, I felt sad because they did not see me, even though I was standing right next to them. They were lost on their mobiles and did not realize what was happening around them at all. They did not even speak to each other because they were only thinking about the games they were playing. Normally, at school, we are best friends and have lots of fun together.

Wer?
Wo?
Was machen die beiden?
Was denken die beiden?

After waiting for a moment, I called them and they recognized my voice and looked up at me. They were surprised, but then smiled at me and told me they were sorry for not seeing me. They got up and we went to the next ice-cream corner and enjoyed the sunny afternoon together.

Was passiert als Nächstes?

In the end, it was a great afternoon, but the three of us will try to pay more attention to the world around us and less to our mobile phones in the future.

Schluss

240 words

The importance of travelling

✎ Hinweis: Bei dem Schreibwettbewerb geht es um das Thema „Die Bedeutung des Reisens". Überlege dir, warum das Reisen für dich wichtig ist, und vergiss nicht, in deinem Text vier der fünf Fragen zu beantworten.

Travelling is a very important part of my life. Like many families, my sister, my parents and I always spend two weeks in a foreign country during the summer holidays.

Einleitung

Normally we start planning in winter because we think it is important to have a good plan. That way, we can relax during the journey and forget all stress at home. Besides, I love having so much time to look forward to the journey.

Wichtige Aspekte beim Reisen

Last summer we visited Austria. You may think that sounds boring, but we had lots of fun. While travelling, all of us need lots of action. And there was a lot of action in Austria: we went hiking, cycling and swimming in clear lakes and rivers. But our biggest adventure was a guided mountain bike trail tour with a great view over the mountains. I had never imagined how beautiful the Alps really are.

Welche Länder?

Spannendstes Erlebnis

For me, travelling means having fun, relaxing and enjoying time with the family. Moreover, by travelling you can learn a lot about other countries, for example about the culture or the language.

Vorteile des Reisens

We have already been to Spain, Croatia and Denmark, for example. Next year, we would like to fly to New York. This has always been

Welche Länder / Orte?

my parents' biggest dream. I am excited about it, too, and maybe I can even practise my English there.

Negative effects of travelling that I can think of are that you must spend lots of money and that it also pollutes the environment. Nachteile des Reisens

However, I am convinced that travelling has more advantages than disadvantages and I would not want to miss it for the world. Schluss

270 words

A Listening Comprehension

Hinweis: Der Hörverstehensteil der Abschlussprüfung 2021 besteht aus drei Teilen. Alle Texte werden zweimal vorgespielt. Du kannst während des Abspielens jederzeit mit deinen Eintragungen beginnen. Im ersten Teil hörst du zwei Nachrichten, der zweite Teil ist eine Umfrage und der dritte Teil ein Interview.

Part One

Hinweis: Lies dir zunächst die Aussagen zu „News Item 1" durch. Dafür hast du 20 Sekunden Zeit. Während des ersten Hörens kannst du bereits mit Bleistift mögliche Antworten ankreuzen. Denke aber daran, dass du deine endgültigen Antworten mit Füller oder Kugelschreiber festhältst. Für jede richtige Antwort bekommst du einen Punkt. Wenn du bei einer Teilaufgabe mehrere Antworten ankreuzt, bekommst du keinen Punkt.

Im ersten „News Item" geht es um das sogenannte „Pancake race" in Olney, Buckinghamshire, eine fast 600 Jahre alte Tradition, bei der Frauen mit einer Bratpfanne in der Hand um die Wette laufen. Deine Aufgabe ist es, zu erkennen, wann das Rennen stattfindet (a), warum das Rennen nach einer Pause während des Zweiten Weltkriegs wieder aufleben konnte (b), welche Voraussetzungen man erfüllen muss, um an dem Rennen teilnehmen zu können (c) und was die Strecke charakterisiert (d). Bevor du „News Item 2" hörst, hast du erneut 20 Sekunden Zeit, dir die Aufgaben durchzulesen. Es geht hier um den Kater Clyde, der sechs Jahre lang vermisst und nach so langer Zeit zu seiner Familie zurückgebracht wurde. Du musst erkennen, nach welchem Ereignis Clyde entlaufen ist (a), wann die Familie Clyde bekommen hat (b), wie der Kater sechs Jahre lang lebte (c) und woran die Besitzerin ihn nach all der Zeit sofort erkannte (d).

News Item 1

a) The pancake race takes place _____ Lent.

- [x] before
- [ ] during
- [ ] after

Hinweis: "The race, which takes place on the day before the beginning of Lent" (Z. 3–5)

b) In 1948, the race was held again after the vicar
- [ ] had cleaned all the cupboards.
- [✓] had discovered some old photographs.
- [ ] came running with a frying pan.

✏ **Hinweis:** *"When he was cleaning out a cupboard, he came across some old photos […] of women running with frying pans." (Z. 10–13)*

c) To take part in the race, you must
- [ ] carry a skirt.
- [ ] be male and over 18.
- [✓] wear something on your head.

✏ **Hinweis:** *"Participants must wear a skirt, a <u>headscarf</u> and carry a frying pan." (Z. 19/20)*
Lass dich von der Antwortmöglichkeit „carry a skirt" nicht veunsichern: das bedeutet nicht „einen Rock anhaben", sondern „einen Rock tragen" im Sinne von „mit sich führen, dabei haben". „Einen Rock anhaben" heißt auf Englisch „to wear a skirt".

d) The race
- [✓] finishes at the church.
- [ ] is about 400 metres long.
- [ ] is about 365 yards long.

✏ **Hinweis:** *"The race is about 400 yards, or about 365 metres, from the marketplace to the church door." (Z. 20–22)*

News Item 2

a) Clyde went missing after his owners had moved
- [ ] away from Bradford-on-Avon.
- [ ] at Halloween.
- [✓] to a new house.

✏ **Hinweis:** *"Clyde escaped and disappeared days after his owners moved to a new home" (Z. 3/4)*

b) Clyde originally came from a rescue centre
- [ ] 6 years ago.
- [✓] 15 years ago.
- [ ] in 2013.

✏ **Hinweis:** *"they had got Clyde […] from a rescue centre 15 years ago." (Z. 12–14)*

c) The black cat had been

  ☐ found inside an old people's home.

  ☐ fed by someone called George.

  ☑ looked after at an old people's home.

Hinweis: "*after having been seen hanging around outside an old people's home […] He was fed by staff and people called him George.*" (Z. 21–24)

d) The owner Mrs Sargeant said she saw it was Clyde because

  ☑ he has shiny eyes.

  ☐ he looks like his sister.

  ☐ he has a microchip.

Hinweis: "*Mrs Sargeant recognised him straight away by his bright eyes.*" (Z. 24–26)

Part Two

Hinweis: In Teil 2 hat eine Reporterin sieben Personen zum Thema Videospiele befragt. Die Aussagen der Befragten sind in Sprechblasen vorgegeben. Du musst die Aussagen den entsprechenden Personen zuordnen. Für jede richtige Zuordnung erhältst du einen Punkt. Beachte, dass am Ende eine Aussage übrig bleibt, weil acht Aussagen vorgegeben sind, aber nur sieben Personen befragt wurden.

Du hast zum Lesen der Aussagen 40 Sekunden Zeit. Unterstreiche Schlüsselwörter in den Sprechblasen, auf die du dich während des Zuhörens konzentrieren kannst.

Kieran	Helena	Nina	Jordan	Mrs Townsend	Annie	Macaulay
C	G	A	D	B	F	H

Hinweise:

zu Kieran: "*I can forget about school stress or any other problems I might have*" (Z. 11/12)

zu Helena: "*I can analyse problems faster and make decisions more quickly.*" (Z. 20/21)

zu Nina: "*they are the ones whose grades suffer*" (Z. 24/25)/"*they forget their homework or are half-dead in the lessons.*" (Z. 27–29)

zu Jordan: "*It really has improved my knowledge of history.*" (Z. 34/35)

zu Mrs Townsend: "*he's losing touch with his children.*" (Z. 42/43)/"*His relationship to my sister has got worse too.*" (Z. 45/46)

zu Annie: "*I think that this is the same skill that young people need to build career networks*" (Z. 52–54)

zu Macaulay: "*first person shooter games can increase aggressive behaviour.*" (Z. 58/59)

Part Three

Hinweis: Der dritte Teil ist ein Interview mit Sunny, einem Einwanderer aus Nigeria, der fast 21 Jahre lang nachts in Londoner Bussen geschlafen hat.
Lies dir die Anweisungen genau durch und ergänze die gesuchten Informationen. Wo nicht anders verlangt, sollst du jeweils nur eine Information pro Tabellenzeile angeben und kannst pro Tabellenzeile einen Punkt erreichen. Machst du mehrere Angaben und ist eine davon falsch, gibt es keinen Punkt. Sprachliche Fehler führen nicht zum Punktabzug, solange der Inhalt verständlich und korrekt ist. Stichpunkte reichen aus, Zahlen musst du nicht ausschreiben.

(1) Sunny's age	**55**
(2) year he came to Britain	**1998**
(3) why he had to leave Nigeria	• **(he had been a) (political) prisoner** • **(he had) campaigned for democracy** • **(he had been given the) death sentence** • **persecution/(he was) persecuted**
(4) why he spent the night on buses	• **buses (were) safer/warmer** • **centres (were often) overcrowded** • **he was homeless**
(5) best place to sleep on a double-decker bus	**downstairs/at the back**
(6) why it was difficult to sleep on a bus (two details)	• **constant movement/movement of the bus** • **(neon) lights** • **noisy travellers** • **humming/sound of (the) engine**
(7) why Sunny did not have the right to stay in the UK	**(he had) no proof that he had lived in the UK/there (for twenty years)./** **(there was) no record of him living there/anywhere (in the UK)**
(8) what a bus driver did to help	**(he) wrote a letter (of support)**
(9) how he feels today	**(he has been very) lucky**

Hinweise:
zu 1: "Sunny, a fifty-five-year-old" (Z. 1/2)
zu 2: "I came to Britain in 1998." (Z. 8)
zu 3: "I was a political prisoner because I had campaigned for democracy. I had been given the death sentence" (Z. 9–11)

E 2021-4

zu 4: "*the London night buses were safer and warmer than the streets and the centres were often overcrowded.*" *(Z. 22–24)*

zu 5: "*the best place to sleep was downstairs at the back of the bus.*" *(Z. 34–36)*

zu 6: "*It is still not easy to sleep, though – the constant movement of the bus, the neon lights, the noisy travellers and the humming sound of the engine all make sleeping quite difficult.*" *(Z. 38–42)*

zu 7: "*I didn't have any proof that I had lived in the UK for over twenty years. There was no record of me living anywhere.*" *(Z. 48–51)*

zu 8: "*I asked one of the friendliest bus drivers to write a letter of support for me*" *(Z. 53/54)*

zu 9: "*I have been very lucky.*" *(Z. 62/63)*

B Reading Comprehension

1. Banksy

Hinweis: Du musst die Überschriften (A–G) den Abschnitten eines Textes (1–5) zuordnen. Es gibt sieben Überschriften, aber nur fünf Textabschnitte, deshalb bleiben zwei Überschriften übrig. Für jede richtige Zuordnung bekommst du einen Punkt.

Lies zunächst die Textabschnitte durch und suche nach Schlüsselwörtern, die du so oder in ähnlicher Weise (z. B. in Form von Synonymen) in den Überschriften wiederfindest. Achte bei der Zuordnung darauf, dass die Überschrift alle Aspekte des Textabschnittes berücksichtigt.

part of the text	❶	❷	❸	❹	❺
heading	E	F	G	A	C

Hinweise:

zu 1: An den Formulierungen „political artist", „provocative work" und „criticism of society and its conditions" erkennst du, dass es hier um politische Botschaften geht. Dass Banksy ein anonymer Künstler ist und sich seine Werke in einer legalen Grauzone bewegen, wird zwar jeweils kurz erwähnt, es sind aber nicht die Hauptthemen dieses Abschnitts, daher passen die Überschriften A und B nicht.

zu 2: Der zweite Textabschnitt befasst sich mit Banksys Motiven, u. a. Affen und Ratten – letztere sind sein Lieblingsmotiv und der gesamte zweite Teil des Abschnitts beschäftigt sich damit.

zu 3: Der dritte Abschnitt handelt von Fälschungen (auf Englisch „forgeries") von 10 Pfund-Scheinen, die Banksy erstellt und in Umlauf gebracht hat.

zu 4: Hier geht es um Banksys wachsenden Erfolg („success") und Reichtum. Banksy bereut nicht seine Werke, sondern nur die Tatsache, dass diese finanziell so wertvoll und kommerziell so erfolgreich sind, daher ist Überschrift D falsch.
zu 5: Hier wird erklärt, dass Banksy nach wie vor seine wahre Identität geheim hält und dass schon mehrfach versucht wurde, herauszufinden, wer er ist, allerdings ohne eindeutiges Ergebnis.

2. **Young people and working attitudes**

   Hinweis: Hier musst du jeweils aus vier Antwortmöglichkeiten diejenige ankreuzen, die den Satz richtig vervollständigt. Die Sätze sind chronologisch angeordnet, d. h., die Antwort zu a) findest du zu Beginn des Textes, die zu b) etwas weiter unten im Text usw.
   Lies dir zunächst den Text einmal komplett durch. Wenn du beim ersten Lesen nicht alles verstehst, ist das nicht schlimm. Sobald du dich genauer mit den einzelnen Abschnitten beschäftigst, lässt sich vieles aus dem Zusammenhang erschließen.
   Markiere Schlüsselwörter in den Sätzen, den du vervollständigen musst, und dann auch in den Textstellen, die die dazugehörigen Antworten enthalten. So findest du die entsprechenden Stellen schnell wieder, wenn du deine Lösungen am Ende noch einmal überprüfst.

   a) The number of teenagers working on Saturdays has _____ in the last 20 years.
      - ☐ grown
      - ☐ doubled
      - ☐ increased
      - ☑ decreased

      Hinweis: "The number of teenagers working in Saturday jobs has almost halved in the past 20 years." (Z. 1)

   b) One in four 16- and 17-year-olds
      - ☐ works online.
      - ☐ has never worked.
      - ☑ has a traditional job.
      - ☐ stacks shelves.

      Hinweis: "Only one in four 16- and 17-year-olds takes up paid traditional work" (Z. 4)

   c) A typical Saturday job will bring in about _____ a month.
      - ☐ £ 20
      - ☐ £ 48
      - ☑ £ 250
      - ☐ £ 2,000

Hinweis: *"the £250 a typical teenager would earn monthly working Saturdays." (Z. 9)*

d) Many teenagers do not want to start working too soon because they
- [ ] want to postpone their studies.
- [✓] want to concentrate on their education.
- [ ] will not be prepared for working life.
- [ ] will not work for long enough.

Hinweis: *"many young people [...] want to focus more strongly on studies." (Z. 10/11)*

e) Not having a Saturday job can create problems because teenagers
- [✓] have no work experience.
- [ ] have no money.
- [ ] are not prepared for online work.
- [ ] struggle with long-term milestones.

Hinweis: *"This lack of work experience can create longer-term problems" (Z. 14)*

f) As a teenager, the London mayor worked
- [ ] in a food shop.
- [ ] in a restaurant.
- [✓] at a construction site.
- [ ] at a hairdresser's.

Hinweis: *"the London mayor Sadiq Khan worked on a building site" (Z. 17/18)*

g) According to Amy Leonard, young people starting work
- [ ] know how to behave in a working environment.
- [ ] can work in a team at the workplace.
- [ ] can explain the world of work.
- [✓] need help to adjust to the workplace.

Hinweis: *"It's also about explaining the world of work and helping young adults to develop the confidence to take that next step from education into work." (Z. 26/27)*

h) Many _____ think school leavers are not prepared properly for work.
- [ ] executives
- [✓] employers
- [ ] researchers
- [ ] entrepreneurs

Hinweis: *"almost half of the employers believe that young people leaving school, college or university are not ready for work." (Z. 28/29)*

i) Online work allows young people to
- ☑ be more flexible.
- ☐ try a traditional job.
- ☐ work locally.
- ☐ develop key skills.

Hinweis: "they found this line of work more flexible" (Z. 31)

k) A third of all unemployed people
- ☐ are socially disadvantaged.
- ☐ have always worked.
- ☐ have bought and sold clothes online.
- ☑ have never had a job.

Hinweis: "a third of people who are currently out of work have never been employed" (Z. 33/34)

3. Molly's first day at work

Hinweis: Lies den Romanauszug zunächst vollständig durch, damit du weißt, worum es geht. Lies anschließend die Fragen, damit du beim zweiten Lesen die Textstellen markieren kannst, die die Antworten beinhalten.
Du musst nicht in vollständigen Sätzen antworten. Für sprachliche Fehler gibt es keinen Punktabzug, sofern man versteht, was gemeint ist und deine Aussage inhaltlich richtig ist.

a) Her hands shake / start shaking.

Hinweis: "Especially because my hands are shaking" (Z. 4)

b) (You can buy) tablecloths / (painted) plates / (letterpress) notecards / (handcrafted artisan) jewelry.

Hinweis: "it looks like Zooey Deschanel exploded into five thousand tablecloths and painted plates and letterpress notecards." (Z. 5/6), "a bissel of handcrafted artisan jewelry." (Z. 9)

c) Her voice comes out comically high. / She sounds squeaky (when she talks).

Hinweis: "my voice comes out comically high. Squeaky Molly." (Z. 12)

d) – They are (both) very nice.
  They are (both) tall.
  They are (both) big-boned.
- – They (both) wear / have thick-framed glasses.
- – They (both) have (brightly coloured / brightly colored / amazingly intricate) tattoos on their arms.
- – Ari is bald and Deborah has wild black hair.

🖊 *Hinweis:* "She's intensely nice. They both are." (Z. 14/15), "they're a perfect matched set: tall and big-boned, with thick-framed glasses. Ari's bald, and Deborah has this kind of wild black hair" (Z. 17–19), "they both have these brightly colored, amazingly intricate tattoos" (Z. 20/21)

e) Because they are (about) the same age.

🖊 *Hinweis:* "You guys are the same age. I bet you have a lot in common." (Z. 33)

f) – Reid wears a Lord of the Rings shirt and electric white sneakers./Reid is tall/big/husky.
   – Deborah and Ari are/seem punk rock/badass/are not into Lord of the Rings/have tattoos.

🖊 *Hinweis: Du musst ein Merkmal von Reid und ein Merkmal von Deborah und Ari nennen und den Unterschied zwischen Reid und seinen Eltern deutlich machen. Nur dann bekommst du zwei Punkte. An folgenden Textstellen findest du die gesuchten Informationen:* "He's tall and kind of big, in that way people describe as husky." (Z. 28), "His shirt has a map of Middle Earth on it. And his sneakers are so electric white" (Z. 28/29), "Punkrock and badass and not into Lord of the Rings" (Z. 41/42), "They have tattoos" (Z. 42).

g) They make you feel comfortable and relaxed, so you are willing to talk about personal things – even though they are strangers./They give you the feeling that they'd listen to you and be interested in everything you say.

🖊 *Hinweis: Auch wenn die Antwort nicht direkt im Text enthalten ist, erklärt Molly, warum sie Deborah und Ari so wahrnimmt:* "They're nice in the way therapists are – like, you get the impression they'd be up for hearing your thoughts about life and humanity." (Z. 16/17). *Daraus geht hervor, dass die beiden sehr offen, interessiert und warmherzig sind und dass man sich in ihrer Gegenwart schnell wohlfühlt und öffnet.*

h) She wants to appear competent/professional on her first day at work./She does not want to lose her job./She wants to make a good impression on her first day of work./She does not want to admit that she has forgotten how to use it.

🖊 *Hinweis: Der gesamte Text beschreibt, wie sehr sich Molly über ihre Anstellung bei Deborah und Ari freut, wie sehr sie die beiden bewundert und wie aufgeregt sie ist. Deborah erwartet, dass Molly sich aus dem Vorstellungsgespräch daran erinnert, wie man die Kasse bedient (vgl. Z. 22/23:* "Hmm, so I guess we probably went over most of this stuff at the interview. You remember how to use the register?"), *daher möchte Molly sie nicht enttäuschen, zumal es die allererste Aufgabe ist, die sie in ihrem Job erhält.*

C Use of Language

1. Mediation – Interview with a YouTuber

Hinweis: In der Mediation sollst du zwischen Sabine und der US-amerikanischen YouTuberin vermitteln.

Achte immer genau auf die jeweils geforderte Zielsprache, die in eckigen Klammern angegeben ist. Du musst dabei nicht alles Wort für Wort übersetzen, sondern nur die wichtigsten Informationen. Oft gibt es mehr als eine Möglichkeit, etwas auszudrücken.

Beachte, dass zwischen Hauptaussagen und weiteren Aspekten unterschieden wird. Die Hauptaussage musst du immer in die andere Sprache übertragen. Nennst du die Hauptaussage nicht, wird der jeweilige Gesprächsbeitrag mit null Punkten bewertet, selbst wenn die Nebenaspekte richtig sind.

Damit du dich gut zurechtfindest, sind in den Lösungen die Hauptaussagen mit Sternchen (*) gekennzeichnet. Außerdem ist in Klammern angegeben, für welche Aussagen du Punkte erhältst.

Gibst du Antworten in der falschen Sprache, bekommst du ebenfalls keinen Punkt. Verwendest du eine falsche Perspektive (egal ob einmalig oder mehrfach), wird dir von der Gesamtpunktzahl der Mediation einmalig ein Punkt abgezogen.

Kommentare wie „Das hätte ich jetzt nicht erwartet", „Das wundert mich" oder „Das klingt sehr überzeugend" sind keine zentralen Informationen, daher brauchst du sie nicht zu übertragen.

Sabine:	Nochmals danke, dass du mir hilfst! Ich bin ganz aufgeregt. OK, frag doch bitte als Erstes, wie lange sie schon Videos macht und warum sie damit überhaupt angefangen hat.
Du [Englisch]:	**How long have you been making (YouTube) videos (1*) and why did you start in the first place? (1*)**
YouTuberin:	Ah, for quite a while now. I started my YouTube channel about four years ago. And I didn't think of money or fame, as people sometimes think. I did it because I've always loved to entertain. I guess it is just the right thing for me to do.
Du [Deutsch]:	**Sie macht das seit ungefähr vier Jahren. (1*) Sie hat es schon immer geliebt, zu unterhalten, deshalb hat sie (damit) angefangen. (1*) Als sie anfing, ging es ihr aber nicht um Geld oder Ruhm./Das passt einfach zu ihr. (1)**
Sabine:	Ah, so lange schon! Das hätte ich jetzt nicht erwartet. Kann sie denn davon leben?
Du [Englisch]:	**Can you make a living doing this/from it? (1*)**
YouTuberin:	Haha, I can only dream of that. I do it in addition to my regular job.

Du [Deutsch]:	**Nein, sie macht es zusätzlich zu ihrem normalen Beruf. (1*)**
Sabine:	Oh, das wundert mich, dass sie das zeitlich hinbekommt. Ich habe gelesen, dass die Produktion von Videos sehr zeitaufwendig ist. Was motiviert sie denn dann, immer neue Inhalte zu produzieren?
Du [Englisch]:	**What motivates/drives you to produce new content all the time? (1*)**
YouTuberin:	What drives me? That's really easy to explain! I do it because it is great fun. For example, I really enjoy the process of coming up with ideas, filming, and editing. Seeing the responses from my viewers is what really keeps me going.
Du [Deutsch]:	**Sie macht es, weil es ihr Spaß macht. (1*) Der Prozess, Ideen zu entwickeln, zu filmen und zu schneiden macht ihr (wirklich/große) Freude. (1) Die Reaktionen ihres Publikums zu sehen motiviert sie, weiterzumachen. (1*)**
Sabine:	Toll! Das klingt sehr überzeugend! Ich kann ihre Begeisterung spüren. Frage sie doch mal nach typischen Reaktionen ihrer Fans. Ich finde das sehr interessant.
Du [Englisch]:	**How do your fans typically react? (1*)**
YouTuberin:	I love communicating with my viewers. Some people have sent me pictures of drawings they've made for me. Many send me fanmail telling me how much my videos have inspired them to try something new. It's times like those that make my efforts worthwhile.
Du [Deutsch]:	**Ihre Fans schicken ihr Bilder von Zeichnungen, die sie für sie angefertigt haben. (1) Sie schicken ihr Fanpost und berichten davon, wie ihre Videos sie dazu inspiriert haben, etwas Neues auszuprobieren. (1*)**
Sabine:	Faszinierend. Das zeigt, wie wichtig ihre Videos für sie sind. Das war ein sehr informatives Gespräch. Danke ihr bitte dafür und sage ihr, dass sie heute einen neuen Fan gewonnen hat.
Du [Englisch]:	**Thank you for your time and Sabine says that you gained a new fan today. (1*)**
YouTuberin:	No problem, that was fun! Great to hear – see you on YouTube then. Bye and take care.

2. Words and structures – How Garfield telephones ended up on French beaches

🖋 *Hinweis: Diese Aufgabe überprüft deine Kenntnisse in Wortschatz und Grammatik in Form eines Lückentextes. Lies den Text zuerst einmal komplett, bevor du mit der Bearbeitung der Aufgaben beginnst. Für jede Lücke sind vier Antwortmög-*

lichkeiten vorgegeben, die du genau anschauen solltest – oft sind nämlich zwischen den einzelnen Optionen nur kleine Unterschiede. Wenn du dich für eine Antwort entschieden hast, überprüfe deine Wahl noch einmal anhand des Ausschlussverfahrens. Für jede richtige Antwort gibt es einen Punkt.

1.		2.		3.		4.	
☐	When	☑	People	☐	was coming	☐	Of
☐	For	☐	Peoples	☑	were coming	☐	At
☑	Since	☐	People's	☐	are coming	☐	In
☐	Because	☐	Peoples'	☐	will be coming	☑	On
5.		6.		7.		8.	
☐	as	☐	They	☐	out	☐	polluted
☐	unlike	☐	Anybody	☐	of	☐	pollutant
☑	like	☐	Everybody	☑	off	☑	pollution
☐	similar	☑	Nobody	☐	over	☐	polluting
9.		10.					
☑	where	☑	doesn't				
☐	were	☐	don't				
☐	while	☐	hadn't				
☐	who	☐	haven't				

🖋 **Hinweise:**

zu 1: *In diese Lücke passt nur* since*, da es sich um einen Zeitpunkt in der Vergangenheit handelt.* For *steht bei Zeitspannen und passt daher nicht; die anderen beiden Möglichkeiten ergeben keinen grammatikalisch richtigen Satz.*

zu 2: *Das Nomen* people *ist ein Pluralwort und wird mit „Leute", „Menschen" übersetzt. Das Wort* peoples *ist hier falsch, da es „Völker" bedeutet. Die Wörter* People's *und* Peoples' *haben jeweils ein Genitiv-s, aber an diese Stelle passt kein Genitiv.*

zu 3: *Wegen der Zeitangabe* for three decades *und der Vergangenheitsform* no one knew *muss in diese Lücke eine „past tense"-Form. Da das Wort* phones *im Plural steht, ist* were coming *die richtige Lösung.*

zu 4: *Bei Datumsangaben wird immer die Präposition* on *verwendet.*

zu 5: *Das Wort* like *bedeutet „wie (z. B.)" und ist das einzige, das in diesen Satz passt, denn* as *bedeutet „als, wie",* unlike *„unähnlich, anders als" und* similar *„ähnlich".*

zu 6: *In diese Lücke passt inhaltlich nur* Nobody *(„niemand"), da es in dem Text darum geht, dass seit Jahrzehnten niemand genau weiß, wo die Garfield-Telefone herkamen.*

zu 7: *Hier kann nur* off *stehen, da* to fall off *die englische Entsprechung für „herunterfallen" ist.*

zu 8: *Hier passt nur das Nomen* pollution *(„Verschmutzung"). Das Partizip Perfekt* polluted *bedeutet „verschmutzt", das Partizip Präsens* polluting *„verschmutzend" und das Nomen* pollutant *„Schadstoff".*

zu 9: *Da hier ein Ort näher beschrieben wird, kann nur* where *richtig sein. Achtung: Verwechsle nicht* where *(„wo") und* who *(„wer")!*

zu 10: *Die richtige Form ist* doesn't, *da es sich um die dritte Person Singular handelt und da eine „simple present"-Form benötigt wird, weil es um eine allgemeingültige Tatsache geht.*

D Text Production

Hinweis: Im letzten Teil der Prüfung, der Textproduktion, kannst du 25 Punkte, also ein Viertel der Gesamtpunktzahl, erreichen. Du darfst aus zwei Aufgaben eine auswählen: Du kannst entweder einen Text zu dem vorgegebenen Bild oder einen zum Thema „Digital Detox" schreiben.

Für beide Themen gilt die Vorgabe, dass du ungefähr 150 Wörter verwenden und auf mindestens vier der fünf vorgegebenen Fragen eingehen musst.

Neben den Punkten für Inhalt (10 Punkte), Grammatik (5 Punkte) und Wortschatz (5 Punkte) kannst du 5 Punkte für die Organisation deines Textes bekommen. Achte daher darauf, dass dein Text gut strukturiert ist. Es muss ein „roter Faden" durch Einleitung, Hauptteil und Schluss zu erkennen sein und dein Text sollte durch Absätze eine Struktur erhalten.

Im Lösungsvorschlag stehen als Hilfe bei jedem Absatz am Rand kurze Stichpunkte zur Orientierung. Auch wenn du andere Formulierungen oder Argumente verwendet hast, kannst du so vergleichen, ob du deinen Text sinnvoll strukturiert und die wichtigen Aspekte bedacht hast.

Zähle die Wörter, wenn du mit dem Schreiben fertig bist. Wenn dein ganzer Text sinnvoll ist und keine Wiederholungen enthält, darfst du auch mehr als 150 Wörter schreiben. Die Lösungsvorschläge sind ein wenig länger; so erhältst du Anregungen für die inhaltliche Ausgestaltung und für gute Formulierungen, die man immer wieder verwenden kann.

What is the story behind the picture?

Hinweis: Lasse deiner Fantasie freien Lauf! Du musst nur darauf achten, dass du mindestens vier der fünf Fragen beantwortest und das Bild genau anschaust, damit dein Text plausibel ist. Der abgedruckte Text ist nur ein Vorschlag; deine Lösung kann auch dann sehr gut sein, wenn sie inhaltlich davon abweicht.

The couple in this picture are my grandparents, the cutest and happiest couple I have ever known. **Einleitung:** Wer?

Here you can see one of their first selfies. It was taken on our last family holiday to the Alps. Before we got there we had some chaotic weeks because my parents and I had moved to a bigger apartment **Was ist vorher passiert?**

and my grandparents helped us pack our stuff into boxes. While packing I found my old smartphone and it still worked. So I gave it to my grandparents. I showed them how to use it especially for videocalls because our new apartment is further away from theirs and I'll probably see them less now. But what they loved most was taking selfies, so after our move the fun started!

This picture was taken at their favourite place – on top of the moun- tain where my grandfather asked my grandmother to marry him 40 years ago. You can see in their faces how happy they are and I hope they will have many more happy years together. *172 words*

Wo?

Schluss: Wie fühlen sie sich?

Digital detox

/ **Hinweis:** *Stell dir vor, du wettest mit deinem besten Freund oder deiner besten Freundin, dass du es schaffst, zwei Wochen ohne Internet und Handy zu leben. Über- lege dir Antworten auf mindestens vier der Fragen und schreibe dann einen Text über deine Zeit ohne Internet und Handy.*

Here I am, day five of 14 and I am still going strong! I made a bet with my best friend Susie that I can live without the Internet and my phone for two weeks. I have always wanted to make this kind of digital detox and this is my chance.

I really miss chatting with my friends and reading their posts about their feelings and experiences. I am getting used to it but at the be- ginning it was my personal nightmare: I felt bored and had no idea what to do.

However, now I have restructured my days and started some new free time activities: I go to the gym and I often meet friends in per- son. I also read more and play games with my little sister. And it is fun – I feel positive and happy. I am really confident about finishing this challenge. If I lose I will have to invite Susie for dinner, but believe me, I am going to win and it is she who will invite me to dinner! *175 words*

Einleitung

Was vermisse ich am meisten?

Wie verbringe ich die Zeit?

Wie fühle ich mich?

Schluss: Wetteinsatz

A Listening Comprehension

Hinweis: Der Hörverstehensteil der Abschlussprüfung 2022 besteht aus drei Teilen. Alle Texte werden zweimal vorgespielt. Du kannst während des Abspielens jederzeit mit deinen Eintragungen beginnen. Im ersten Teil hörst du zwei Nachrichten, der zweite Teil ist eine Umfrage und Teil 3 ein Interview.

Part One

*Hinweis: Du hast zunächst 20 Sekunden Zeit, dir die Aussagen zu „News Item 1"
durchzulesen. Beim ersten Hören kannst du mit Bleistift mögliche Antworten ankreuzen, aber vergiss nicht, deine endgültigen Antworten mit Füller oder Kugelschreiber
festzuhalten. Jede richtige Antwort ergibt einen Punkt. Wenn du bei einer Teilaufgabe
mehrere Antworten ankreuzt, bekommst du null Punkte.*

*Das erste „News Item" handelt von Versteigerungen, bei denen Gegenstände aus berühmten Hollywood-Filmen erworben werden können. Du musst die Umstände der
ersten Versteigerung herausfinden (a), außerdem musst du herausfinden, wie viel
Geld ein Schwert aus dem Film* Der Herr der Ringe *einbrachte (b), welche Farbe
Dorothys Schuhe im Buch* Der Zauberer von Oz *haben (c) und die Waffe welchen
James-Bond-Darstellers versteigert wurde (d).*

*Bevor du „News Item 2" hörst, hast du noch mal 20 Sekunden Zeit, die vier Aussagen
zu lesen. Es geht um die Insektenart der Zikaden. Du musst beantworten, für wie viele
Jahre diese Insekten unter der Erde leben (a), wann sie an der Oberfläche auftauchen
(b), wo weibliche Zikaden ihre Eier ablegen (c) und was mit ihnen am Ende ihres
Lebens geschieht (d).*

News Item 1

a) MGM Studios started selling famous items from films
   ☐ in 2014.
   ☑ to save money.
   ☐ to Hollywood stars.

   *Hinweis: "in the 1970s [...] the president of MGM Studios decided to auction
   off thousands of items from past films in order <u>to save some money</u>." (Z. 4–7)*

b) At one sale, a weapon from *The Lord of the Rings* made
- ☑ $ 510,000.
- ☐ $ 660,000.
- ☐ $ 256,000.

🖊 **Hinweis:** *"Aragorn's sword from* The Lord of the Rings *was put up for auction. It sold for an amazing $510,000" (Z. 9–11)*
Achtung: Die anderen beiden Summen werden auch genannt, beziehen sich aber auf Schuhe aus *Der Zauberer von Oz ($660,000)* und auf eine Waffe aus James Bond *($256,000).*

c) In the book *The Wizard of Oz*, Dorothy's shoes were originally
- ☑ silver.
- ☐ yellow.
- ☐ red.

🖊 **Hinweis:** *"In the book, which came first, the shoes were actually silver but the colour was changed to ruby red for the film" (Z. 15–17)*

d) In 2020, a gun used by James Bond was purchased by
- ☐ Sean Connery.
- ☐ Dr. P. Walther.
- ☑ an unknown buyer.

🖊 **Hinweis:** *"The buyer wishes to remain anonymous" (Z. 22/23)*

News Item 2

a) The cicadas have been underground for _____ years.
- ☐ 10
- ☑ 17
- ☐ 64

🖊 **Hinweis:** *"which have been underground for the past 17 years" (Z. 6/7)*

b) These insects will appear
- ☐ when the air temperature is 17 °C.
- ☑ at night-time.
- ☐ when it is rainy and windy.

🖊 **Hinweis:** *"The ground temperatures must be 64 degrees Fahrenheit, or 17 degrees Celsius, and it must be a humid night, but free of rain and wind."*
(Z. 8–10)
Hier musst du genau hinhören: Die Antwort „when it is rainy and windy" ist falsch, da es eben keinen Regen und Wind geben darf („free of rain and wind"), und die 17 °C beziehen sich auf die Boden- und nicht auf die Lufttemperatur.

c) The female cicadas lay their eggs

☑ on trees.

☐ underground.

☐ at the end of the summer.

🖊 **Hinweis:** *"the female cicadas will then lay their eggs in the branches of young trees." (Z. 15/16)*

d) At the end of their lives, cicadas

☐ feed on plant roots.

☐ burrow into the soil.

☑ are eaten by other animals.

🖊 **Hinweis:** *"their parents die and become a tasty treat for cats, dogs, birds, and even for some people." (Z. 21/22)*

Part Two

🖊 **Hinweis:** *In Teil 2 werden sieben Personen zum Thema „The royal family" befragt. Die Aussagen stehen in Sprechblasen und du musst sie den richtigen Personen zuordnen. Für jede richtige Zuordnung erhältst du einen Punkt. Beachte, dass eine Aussage zu viel ist und niemandem zugeordnet werden kann.*
Du hast 40 Sekunden Zeit, um die Aussagen zu lesen. Unterstreiche Schlüsselwörter in den Sprechblasen, auf die du dich während des Zuhörens konzentrieren kannst.

Jeanette	Irene	Dominic	Leo	Alice	Henry	Dave
B	H	E	D	G	A	F

🖊 **Hinweise:**
zu Jeanette: *"I don't think they do enough for the money they get from the government." (Z. 9–11)*
zu Irene: *"there are a lot of depressing things going on in the world right now and the royals bring some glamour and sparkle into our lives." (Z. 20–22)*
zu Dominic: *"They are a part of our history and define us as a nation." (Z. 28/29)/ "The royal family represents stability and gives us a sense of identity." (Z. 31/32)*
zu Leo: *"The work they do for charities is essential." (Z. 40/41)*
zu Alice: *"but at the end of the day, it was £1.24 per person in the UK. So, not giving them this money anymore doesn't make the ordinary man any richer." (Z. 48–51)*
zu Henry: *"This interest in the royal family generates a lot of money and jobs. Over 2.7 million tourists visited Buckingham Palace and Windsor Castle last year, bringing in more than 550 million pounds." (Z. 56–60)*
zu Dave: *"Although the Queen is the head of the state, she does not run the country" (Z. 63/64)*

Part Three

🖋 **Hinweis:** *Im dritten Teil wird Julian Musgrove, Mitarbeiter der UK Food Group, zum Thema Essensverschwendung interviewt.*

Lies die Aufgabenstellung sorgfältig und ergänze die gesuchten Informationen. Du sollst in jeder Tabellenzeile nur eine Information angeben und kannst dafür einen Punkt erhalten. Wenn du mehrere Angaben machst, von denen eine falsch ist, erhältst du keinen Punkt. Du kannst Stichpunkte schreiben und musst Zahlen nicht ausschreiben. Sprachliche Fehler führen nicht zum Punktabzug, solange der Inhalt verständlich und korrekt ist.

(1) who Julian works for	**UK Food Group**
(2) amount of water needed to grow one apple	**125 litres**
(3) what food waste produces	• **greenhouse gas** • **methane** • **biogas** • **dangerous gas**
(4) where the majority of UK food waste comes from	**homes / households**
(5) positive effect of food waste if properly recycled	**It creates a biogas / energy / electricity.**
(6) what you can do with the energy generated from one banana skin	**(You can) charge a smart phone (twice).**
(7) one tip to reduce food waste at home	• **(write) a meal plan** • **only buy what you need** • **freeze food**
(8) what a 'use-by' date means	• **It's about safety.** • **Food is not safe to eat after this date.** • **It's not eatable anymore.**
(9) how you freeze eggs	**(You must) crack and beat them first.**
(10) what some supermarkets do with unsold food	**(They) donate it (to charities / food banks.)**

🖋 *Hinweise:*
zu 1: "Julian Musgrove, who works for the UK Food Group." (Z. 5/6)
zu 2: "One apple needs an average of 125 litres of water." (Z. 14/15)
zu 3: "Food waste also produces the dangerous greenhouse gas methane." (Z. 21–23)

zu 4: "In the UK, most food waste comes from our homes." (Z. 30/31)

zu 5: "But we can use this food waste to create energy. [...] if your food waste is recycled properly, it [...] produces a biogas which can generate electricity." (Z. 38–43)

zu 6: "The energy created by recycling one banana skin can fully charge a smart phone twice!" (Z. 44/45)

zu 7: "I recommend that you write a meal plan for the week and only buy what you need." (Z. 48/49)

zu 8: "'Use-by' is about safety and food isn't safe to eat after this date." (Z. 51–53)

zu 9: "Most foods can be frozen – even eggs if you crack and beat them first." (Z. 59–61)

zu 10: "Some supermarkets donate unsold food to charities." (Z. 65/66)

B Reading Comprehension

1. "Go, Captain Tom!"

✔ Hinweis: Im ersten Teil des Leseverstehens geht es darum, die Überschriften A–G den Abschnitten des Textes zuzuordnen. Es gibt sieben Überschriften, aber nur fünf Textabschnitte. Für jede richtige Zuordnung bekommst du einen Punkt. Lies zunächst die Textabschnitte durch und suche nach Schlüsselbegriffen, die sich in den Überschriften wiederfinden. Achte bei der Zuordnung darauf, dass die Überschrift alle Aspekte des jeweiligen Textabschnitts berücksichtigt.

part of the text	❶	❷	❸	❹	❺
Heading	F	D	G	B	C

✔ Hinweise:

zu 1: Dieser Textabschnitt beschreibt, wie der 99-jährige Thomas Moore 100 Runden in seinem Garten ging, um während der Covid-19-Pandemie Geld für das britische Gesundheitswesen zu sammeln. Lass dich nicht von dem Wort gripped verunsichern, das sowohl in der ersten Zeile des Textes als auch in Überschrift A vorkommt. Sie passt hier nicht, da es im ersten Abschnitt hauptsächlich um Captain Toms Vorhaben geht und nicht um die Pandemie an sich.

zu 2: Der gesamte Abschnitt befasst sich mit der militärischen Karriere von Thomas Moore: Er schloss sich 1940 der Britischen Armee an, stieg bis zum Hauptmann (captain) auf und schätzte sich glücklich, den Zweiten Weltkrieg unversehrt überlebt zu haben. Wichtig ist hier auch, dass von einem Auslandseinsatz („abroad") nirgends die Rede ist (es wird nur „Cornwall" erwähnt).

zu 3: In Abschnitt 3 geht es um Captain Toms Familienleben von der Kindheit bis ins hohe Alter.

zu 4: Textabschnitt 4 zeigt auf, dass Captain Tom nach einer eigenen Erkrankung dem medizinischen Personal im Krankenhaus sehr dankbar war ("gratitude" = Dankbarkeit) und ihm etwas zurückgeben wollte, um den Kampf gegen das Coronavirus zu unterstützen.

zu 5: Hier werden der Ruhm und alle Ehren beschrieben, die Captain Tom zuteil-wurden: Er wurde durch seine Challenge weltbekannt, brachte ein sehr erfolgreiches Lied heraus, wurde zum Ritter geschlagen und nach seinem Tod mit Glockengeläut und Feuerwerk geehrt.

2. Soccer

Hinweis: Hier ist immer nur eine der vier Antworten richtig. Die Reihenfolge der Aufgaben entspricht der Reihenfolge, in der im Text die Informationen gegeben werden.

Du solltest den Text einmal ganz lesen, bevor du mit dem Bearbeiten der Aufgaben anfängst. Wenn du auf Anhieb nicht alles verstehst, lass dich nicht verunsichern. Wenn du dich intensiver mit den einzelnen Abschnitten beschäftigst, lässt sich vieles aus dem Zusammenhang erschließen.

Unterstreiche Schlüsselwörter sowohl in den zu vervollständigenden Sätzen als auch im Text. Auf diese Weise findest du die entsprechenden Textstellen schnell wieder, wenn du die Lösungen am Ende noch einmal überprüfst.

a) The birthplace of soccer as we know it today is
   - [✓] Britain.
   - [ ] China.
   - [ ] Rome.
   - [ ] Greece.

   Hinweis: "the birthplace of modern soccer is Britain" (Z. 2/3)

b) In former times, folk football was played to
   - [ ] develop ball games.
   - [ ] develop ball rules.
   - [ ] celebrate special customs.
   - [✓] celebrate the new season.

   Hinweis: "to celebrate the return of spring" (Z. 7)

c) Images suggest that the games were played
   - [ ] exactly like rugby.
   - [ ] with the hands only.
   - [✓] with all needed means.
   - [ ] by only a small number of players.

Hinweis: "Images [...] suggest that there was a huge number of players who could move the ball by any means necessary" (Z. 9/10)

d) During the competition, many people
- [ ] scored goals for their villages.
- [ ] left the chaotic contest.
- [✓] were injured.
- [ ] managed to be clever.

Hinweis: "These games involved full body contact and often turned bloody." (Z. 13/14)

e) _____ attempted to abolish the game in Ashbourne.
- [ ] Derbyshire
- [✓] The police
- [ ] Fierce clashes
- [ ] Some tourists

Hinweis: "In Ashbourne in Derbyshire [...] the police attempted to forbid the game" (Z. 16/17)

f) Monarchs wanted to _____ their men's fighting techniques.
- [✓] increase
- [ ] prove
- [ ] show
- [ ] decrease

Hinweis: "Kings and Queens wanted their men to improve their fighting skills" (Z. 20)

g) At respected schools, students played football according to _____ rules.
- [ ] ordinary
- [✓] varying
- [ ] noble
- [ ] privileged

Hinweis: "none of them was ready to play by the rules of someone else's school because each school had its own variations." (Z. 24/25)

h) With the Cambridge Rules, football became _____ rugby.
- [ ] connected to
- [ ] similar to
- [✓] different from
- [ ] equal to

Hinweis: "This was the first attempt to distance football from its shared roots with rugby" (Z. 26/27)

i) Many factory workers could
    ☐ play football all Saturday.
    ☐ attend matches every afternoon.
    ☐ be kept from work by playing the exciting game.
    ☑ play football in the afternoon at weekends.

    Hinweis: "Industrial workers increasingly had Saturday afternoons off [...] So many began to watch and play the exciting game of football." (Z. 28–30)

k) The word soccer was formed by
    ☐ adding one letter to a word.
    ☐ shortening two words.
    ☐ using a shortened form of a letter.
    ☑ shortening letters of a word and adding others.

    Hinweis: "students at Oxford University created a slang word for the word 'association'. They shortened it to 'SOC' and added 'ER', so the word 'soccer' was finally created." (Z. 34–36)

3. Preparing for a date

Hinweis: Lies den Romanauszug einmal komplett, bevor du anfängst, die Fragen zu beantworten. Lies dann konzentriert die Fragen und markiere beim zweiten Lesen des Textes die Stellen, an denen die Antworten stehen.
Du brauchst keine vollständigen Sätze zu schreiben. Für sprachliche Fehler gibt es keinen Punktabzug, sofern deine Aussage inhaltlich richtig und verständlich ist.

a) Trevor needs to up his game./Trevor cannot go to the dance looking the way he does./Trevor has a date.
    Hinweis: "because he has a date" (Einleitung), "You need to up your game" (Z. 1/2), "You cannot go to the dance looking the way you look" (Z. 2)

b) She gives him money/2,000 rand.
    Hinweis: "She finally relented and gave me 2,000 rand" (Z. 5)

c) You only buy one expensive item and the rest must be basic, good-looking quality stuff.
    Hinweis: "The trick to looking rich [...] is to have one expensive item, and for the rest of the things you get basic, good-looking quality stuff." (Z. 7/8)

d) – black pants
    – suede/square-toed shoes
    – a cream-white sweater/a knitted sweater
    – a (black) leather jacket
    Hinweis: "we bought a calf-length black leather jacket [...] Then we finished the outfit with a pair of simple black pants, suede square-toed shoes, and a cream-white knitted sweater." (Z. 8–11)

e) He talks to some girls from his street.
   🖉 *Hinweis: "and we went to talk to some girls from his street" (Z. 16/17).*

f) His hair must be relaxed./His hair is like sheep's wool.
   🖉 *Hinweis: "I can't work with this sheep" (Z. 26), "You have to relax it." (Z. 28)*

g) She says he looks like a girl/his hair looks too pretty.
   🖉 *Hinweis: "it is way too pretty. You do look like a girl." (Z. 45)*

You cannot find the answers to the following questions directly in the text:

h) She is keen for her son to go to the dance/to look good at the dance.
   🖉 *Hinweis: Trevors Mutter zögert erst, ihm Geld für sein Schulball-Outfit zu geben (vgl. Z. 4/5). Ihr Einlenken zeigt, dass es ihr wichtig ist, dass ihr Sohn mit gutem Gefühl und angemessen gekleidet zum Schulball gehen kann.*

i) (He realizes that) women go through a lot of trouble to look good.
   🖉 *Hinweis: Im zweiten Salon werden Trevor die Haare geglättet und die Prozedur ist schmerzhaft. Er ist der einzige Mann im Salon und bekommt dadurch einen Einblick in das, was Frauen durchmachen, um gut auszusehen (vgl. auch Z. 36: "It was a window into what women experience to look good on a regular basis.").*

C Use of Language

1. Mediation – Hitchhiking USA

🖉 *Hinweis: In der Mediation sollst du zwischen Jason, einem Anhalter in den USA, und deinen Eltern dolmetschen.*
Achte immer genau auf die jeweils geforderte Zielsprache, die in eckigen Klammern angegeben ist.
Du musst nicht alles Wort für Wort übersetzen und auch nicht immer vollständige Sätze schreiben. Manchmal gibt es mehr als eine Möglichkeit, etwas auszudrücken.
Du bekommst keine Punkte abgezogen, wenn du sprachliche Fehler machst, es sei denn, die Fehler machen deine Aussage unverständlich.
Beachte, dass bei der Mediation zwischen Hauptaussagen und weiteren Aussagen unterschieden wird. Die Hauptaussage musst du immer in die andere Sprache übertragen. Nennst du die Hauptaussage nicht, so wird der jeweilige Gesprächsbeitrag mit null Punkten bewertet, selbst wenn die Nebenaussagen richtig sind. Damit du dich gut zurechtfindest, sind in den Lösungen die Hauptaussagen mit

einem Sternchen (*) gekennzeichnet, wenn ein Gesprächsbeitrag mehrere Aussagen enthält. Außerdem ist in Klammern angegeben, für welche Aussagen du Punkte erhältst.

Gibst du Antworten in der falschen Sprache, bekommst du ebenfalls keinen Punkt. Halbe Punkte werden nicht vergeben.

Achte auf die Perspektive (Jason, Mutter, Vater). Verwendest du eine falsche Perspektive (egal ob einmalig oder mehrfach), wird dir von der Gesamtpunktzahl der Mediation einmalig ein Punkt abgezogen.

Persönliche Kommentare wie „Ich habe das als Jugendliche auch gemacht" oder „Mir wäre das zu gefährlich" gehören nicht zu den wichtigsten Informationen und du kannst sie deswegen weglassen.

Jason:	Thanks a lot for giving me a lift. I really appreciate it. It's pretty hot out there today and I had been waiting for about two hours already.
Du [Deutsch]:	**Er ist sehr dankbar, dass wir ihn mitnehmen. (1*) Er hat schon etwa zwei Stunden in der Hitze gewartet. (1)**
Mutter:	Keine Ursache! Ich bin, als ich jünger war, auch per Anhalter durch halb Europa gefahren. Allerdings dachte ich immer, dass das in den USA illegal ist. Frag ihn doch bitte mal danach.
Du [Englisch]:	**Isn't it illegal to hitchhike (in the United States)? (1)**
Jason:	Yes and no. It's illegal to stand on the side of a major highway and stop cars because it is a danger to other drivers on the road. However, standing at the entrance before a highway is legal in most states.
Du [Deutsch]:	**Es ist illegal, am Rand der Autobahnen/Highways zu stehen und Autos anzuhalten. (1*) Aber in den meisten Bundesstaaten darf man an den Einfahrten zu den Autobahnen stehen. (1*)**
Vater:	Also, ich würde das niemals machen. Man liest so viel über die Gefahren und man weiß nie, wer einen da mitnimmt. Denkt er nicht, dass es gefährlich ist?
Du [Englisch]:	**Don't you think it's dangerous? (1)**
Jason:	Before I started, I was told numerous times that I would have to be careful. Based on my own experience, I can say that you don't have to worry too much. Most of the people I met were friendly, fascinating and full of entertaining stories.
Du [Deutsch]:	**Er hat die Erfahrung gemacht, dass man sich nicht zu viele Sorgen machen muss. (1*) Die meisten Menschen, die er getroffen hat, waren freundlich, faszinierend und hatten viele unterhaltsame Geschichten zu erzählen. (1)**

Vater:	Na, das klingt jetzt aber fast zu schön, um wahr zu sein. Er muss doch sicher einiges beachten, damit er sicher unterwegs ist. Frag ihn doch mal nach den wichtigsten Sicherheitsregeln, die er beachtet.
Du [Englisch]:	**What are the most important safety rules? (1)**
Jason:	Well, you have to be prepared for everything, really. I think it's important to look confident, so I always look drivers in the eye and smile as they pass. Also, I don't get into every car that stops for me – I trust my instincts. Most importantly, I always snap a quick photo of the back of the car and send it to my twitter account.
Du [Deutsch]:	**Er sagt, es ist wichtig, selbstbewusst zu wirken, deshalb schaut er den Fahrern immer in die Augen und lächelt sie an. / Außerdem steigt er nicht in jedes haltende Auto ein und vertraut auf seine Instinkte. (1) Am wichtigsten ist, dass er immer ein Foto vom Heck des Autos macht und an sein Twitterkonto / seinen Twitteraccount schickt. (1*)**
Mutter:	Das ist mir gerade alles viel zu ernst hier! Ich habe damals auch nur tolle Menschen getroffen und die lustigsten Sachen erlebt. Frage ihn bitte, was bisher sein lustigstes Erlebnis war.
Du [Englisch]:	**What has been your funniest experience so far? (1)**
Jason:	Oh my gosh, that was only two days ago. There was the cutest puppy ever, which I got to hold on my lap for the ride. There was, however, a catch to its cuteness. It was the first car trip for the puppy and she was feeling car sick: after a few bends on the road, the car filled with a disgusting smell. We stopped and checked her fur, but fortunately, they were just farts. We had to ride the rest of the way with the windows down …
Du [Deutsch]:	**Das war vor zwei Tagen, als er während der Fahrt einen ganz süßen Welpen auf dem Schoß hatte. (1) Der Welpe war Autofahren nicht gewohnt und pupste deshalb. (1*)**
Alle:	Ha, ha, ha …

2. Words and structures – Record trip to Mount Everest summit

✎ Hinweis: Diese Aufgabe überprüft deine Kenntnisse in Wortschatz und Grammatik in Form eines Lückentextes. Lies den Text einmal sorgfältig, bevor du beginnst, deine Häkchen zu machen. Schau dir auch die vier Antwortmöglichkeiten zu jeder Lücke genau an. Wenn du dich für eine Antwort entschieden hast, überprüfe deine Wahl auch noch einmal anhand des Ausschlussverfahrens. Für jede richtige Antwort bekommst du einen Punkt.

1.		2.		3.		4.	
☐	reaches	☐	words	☑	were	☐	on
☑	has reached	☐	world	☐	was	☐	at
☐	will reach	☐	worlds'	☐	will	☑	in
☐	didn't reach	☑	world's	☐	want	☐	for
5.		**6.**		**7.**		**8.**	
☑	whose	☐	at	☑	head	☐	assist
☐	who	☐	with	☐	tail	☐	assists
☐	who's	☑	for	☐	arm	☐	assisting
☐	what	☐	about	☐	leg	☑	assisted
9.		**10.**		**11.**			
☐	rarely	☑	from	☐	street		
☑	few	☐	by	☐	path		
☐	little	☐	at	☐	alley		
☐	small	☐	with	☑	way		

🖋 *Hinweise:*

zu 1: Das Signalwort recently *verrät dir, dass hier das* Present Perfect *stehen muss, also* has reached.

zu 2: Es fehlt ein Nomen im Genitiv Singular („der höchste Gipfel *der Welt*"), *sodass nur die Form* world's *passt;* worlds' *ist zwar auch Genitiv, aber Plural, und kann daher hier nicht stehen.*

zu 3: Da die beschriebene Handlung in der Vergangenheit stattgefunden hat, muss eine Simple past-*Form stehen. Und da der Satz mit dem Personalpronomen* they *(Plural) eingeleitet wird, wird die Pluralform* were *benötigt und nicht die Singularform* was. Will *und* want *können außerdem ausgeschlossen werden, da nach beiden Verben immer ein Infinitiv folgt.*

zu 4: Bei Jahreszahlen wird immer die Präposition in *verwendet.*

zu 5: Nur das Relativpronomen whose *ist richtig: Es bedeutet „dessen, deren" und danach stehen immer ein oder mehrere Nomen. Nach* who *müsste ein Verb stehen und* who's *(Kurzform für* who is*) und* what *(„was") passen inhaltlich nicht.*

zu 6: In diese Lücke passt nur die Präposition for, *da* essential for *ein feststehender Ausdruck mit der Bedeutung „wesentlich für" ist.*

zu 7: Hier stehen nur Wörter zur Auswahl, die Körperteile bezeichnen. Das Wort head *kann aber auch ein Verb sein und „gehen zu, sich begeben zu" bedeuten, daher passt es in diese Lücke.*

zu 8: Nur die Form assisted (Past Participle) *ist richtig, da hier eine Passivform vorliegt. Zur Erinnerung: Das Passiv besteht immer aus einer Form von* to be *und einem* Past Participle.

zu 9: Übersetzt heißt a few „einige" *und ist somit das passende Adjektiv, das eingesetzt werden muss, um das Nomen* periods *näher zu beschreiben. Das Adverb* rarely *und die Adjektive* little *und* small *(beide bedeuten „klein") können hier nicht stehen.*

zu 10: Der feststehende Ausdruck from far away *bedeutet „aus der Ferne".*
zu 11: Das Nomen way *wird in diesem Fall nicht mit „Weg" übersetzt, sondern mit „Art und Weise". Die anderen Möglichkeiten können also wegen ihrer Bedeutung ausgeschlossen werden.*

D Text Production

✎ *Hinweis: Im letzten Teil der Prüfung, der Textproduktion, hast du eine Wahlmöglichkeit zwischen drei Aufgaben. Du kannst entscheiden, ob du eine Geschichte zu einem der zwei vorgegebenen Bilder oder einen Text zum Thema „The school of the future" schreiben möchtest.*
Die Textproduktion wird mit 25 Punkten, also einem Viertel der Gesamtpunktzahl, bewertet. Neben den Punkten für Inhalt (10), Grammatik (5) und Wortschatz (5) gibt es weitere 5 Punkte für die Organisation deines Textes. Achte deshalb beim Schreiben darauf, deinen Text klar zu strukturieren, d. h. Absätze einzufügen und einen „roten Faden" zu verwenden, der sich durch Einleitung, Hauptteil und Schluss zieht.
Du musst ungefähr 150 Wörter schreiben und in deinem Text mindestens vier der fünf vorgegebenen Fragen bearbeiten.
Zähle abschließend die Wörter. Du darfst die Wortzahl überschreiten, wenn dein Text durchgehend sinnvoll ist und es zu keinen Wiederholungen kommt.

What is the story behind the picture?
✎ *Hinweis: Lass deiner Fantasie freien Lauf und beziehe die Fragen in deinen Text mit ein. Dein Text muss sich nicht auf eine Geburtstagsfeier beziehen, sondern kann auch einen ganz anderen Inhalt haben, wenn er schlüssig ist und zum Bild passt.*

Look, this is me with my two best friends, Tim and Lisa. And guess what: The picture was taken on my birthday! *(Einleitung: Wer?)*
It was my birthday last Wednesday and I wanted to have a little party on Saturday because I did not feel like celebrating during the week. But my two best friends were of a different opinion!
I was doing my homework when the doorbell rang and both surprised me with the funny hats you can see in the picture and with a birthday cake. *(Was ist vorher passiert?)* We sat down in the living room together and talked and took *(Wo?)* selfies to remember these perfect moments of our friendship. We posted them to our story on Instagram so all our other friends could *(Wie fühlen sie sich?)* see how much fun and what a great time we had. I felt very happy in that moment and I am sure that I have the best friends in the world!
After taking and posting the photos we ate the cake, which was very *(Schluss: Was passiert als Nächstes?)* yummy.   *166 words*

E 2022-13

What is the story behind the picture?

*✐ **Hinweis:** Du kannst deine Kreativität voll ausleben, solange du dich auf das Bild beziehst und an die Vorgaben hältst.*

Yes, we made it! All our final exams are done and it is time to celebrate and say goodbye to our school and teachers. And we are arranging a motto-week so that they will not forget us too soon. Each day during this week has a different motto and the picture you can see is day four with the topic "changed genders".

Einleitung: Was ist vorher passiert?

The boys in the picture are from year 8 and are all wearing girls' school uniforms. They are standing in the school yard and most of them feel strange and a bit awkward because they have never worn a skirt before.

Wer?
Wo?
Wie fühlen sie sich?

However, the best will come tomorrow. We have organized that for one day, everyone can come to school without a uniform and wear whatever they want: typical girls' clothes, typical boys' clothes, neutral clothes or a mix! We want to break down gender stereotypes and I am very much looking forward to tomorrow!

Schluss: Was passiert als Nächstes?

156 words

The school of the future

*✐ **Hinweis:** In einem Projekt einer Universität werden Schülerinnen und Schüler gebeten, Ideen für die Schule der Zukunft zu sammeln. Bestimmt fallen dir viele Dinge ein, die man an der heutigen Schule noch verbessern kann oder die zum Beispiel aufgrund des technischen Fortschritts in Zukunft möglich sein könnten. Schreibe deine Ideen dazu auf und orientiere dich dabei an den vorgegebenen Fragen.*

From the point of view of a student I can say we need a new kind of school. Our schools are old-fashioned and I have a lot of ideas for the school of the future.

Einleitung

To start with, the school of the future needs buildings with modern big rooms. In the future, we will not be taught in traditional classrooms anymore but in workplaces for individual and group learning. In future schools there will be more individual learning and teaching so the strengths of each student can be supported. And perhaps we will no longer be taught in subjects, but in topics we really need for life. The school of the future will be digitally equipped, we will work with tablets or laptops and wifi will be available everywhere.

Wie sieht die Schule der Zukunft aus?

Wo lernen die Schüler*innen?

Wie lernen die Schüler*innen?

To make all this come true, we will need good teachers who guide us and evaluate our skills.

Wer unterrichtet?

With this kind of future school, learning will be much more motivating and we will get more skills that are important for our adult lives.

Schluss: Was ist besser als heute?

172 words

E 2022-14

Um dir die Lösungen zur Prüfung 2023 schnellstmöglich zur Verfügung stellen zu können, bringen wir sie in digitaler Form heraus.

Sobald die Original-Prüfungsaufgaben 2023 freigegeben sind, können die dazugehörigen Lösungen als PDF auf der Plattform **MyStark** heruntergeladen werden (Zugangscode vgl. Umschlaginnenseite).

Aktuelle Prüfung

www.stark-verlag.de/mystark

Dein kostenloses
Stärkenprofil

Du wagst dem-
nächst den Schritt
in die Berufswelt,
aber weißt noch
nicht, was du als
Stärken angeben
kannst?
Mit **Aivy** findest du
es auf spielerische
Art heraus.

 **Aivy** ist…

…für dich kostenlos.

…interaktiv und
spielerisch.

…ganz auf deine
Person fokussiert.

Lerne dich
selbst besser
kennen und

**entdecke
deine
Berufung!**

www.stark-verlag.de   **STARK**

Bist du bereit für deinen Einstellungstest?

Hier kannst du testen, wie gut du in einem Einstellungstest zurechtkommen würdest.

1. **Allgemeinwissen**
Der Baustil des Kölner Doms ist dem/der ... zuzuordnen.

a) Klassizismus   b) Romantizismus
c) Gotik   d) Barock

2. **Wortschatz**
Welches Wort ist das?

N O R I N E T K T A Z N O

3. **Grundrechnen**
-11 + 23 - (-1) =

a) 10   b) 11   c) 12   d) 13

4. **Zahlenreihen**
Welche Zahl ergänzt die Reihe logisch?

17 14 7 21 18 9 ?

5. **Buchstabenreihen**
Welche Auswahlmöglichkeit ergänzt die Reihe logisch?

e d f f e g g f h ? ? ?

a) h i j   b) h g i   c) f g h   d) g h i

Lösungen: 1 c; 2 Konzentration; 3 d; 4 27; 5 b

Alles zum Thema Einstellungstests findest du hier:

www.stark-verlag.de   **STARK**

Bei Fragen rund um das
Thema „Bewerbung"
helfen dir unsere Bücher.

www.stark-verlag.de   **STARK**

PRÜFUNGS-ANGST

STOPP DIE PANIK

Mit der Fußsohlen-Methode

Prüfungen können Angst- und Fluchtsituationen sein. Dein Körper schüttet Adrenalin aus und dämpft das Gefühl in den Füßen. Z. B. beim Weglaufen ist es gut, wenn man die Füße nicht spürt. Eine Prüfung ist aber **keine Gefahrensituation**. Signalisiere deinem Körper, dass du nicht weglaufen musst, und bring das Gefühl in deine Füße zurück:

Setze oder stelle dich hin.
Die Füße müssen den **Boden** berühren.

jeden einzelnen **Zeh** bis **groß**. spüre von klein

Erkunde den **Bogen** deines Fußes.

Spüre den **Druck** auf dem Boden.

Schließe jetzt deine Augen und **denke** dich in deine Füße hinein.

Fahre in Gedanken um die **Fersen**.

Dein Körper **fühlt** die Füße wieder und denkt, er sei in keiner Panik-Situation, sondern in **Sicherheit**.

www.stark-verlag.de **STARK**